SKY HIGH

LAND'S END

AND THE PENWITH COAST

PHOTOGRAPHY BY JASON HAWKES

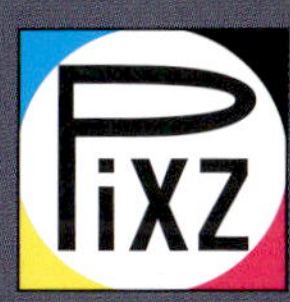

First published in Great Britain in 2009

British Library Cataloguing-in-Publication Data
A CIP record for this title is available from the British Library

ISBN 978 1 906887 49 0

PiXZ Books
Halsgrove House, Ryelands Industrial Estate,
Bagley Road, Wellington, Somerset TA21 9PZ
Tel: 01823 653777
Fax: 01823 216796
email: sales@halsgrove.com

An imprint of Halstar Ltd, part of the Halsgrove group of companies
Information on all Halsgrove titles is available at: www.halsgrove.com

Printed and bound by Grafiche Flaminia, Italy

Introduction

The coastline at the westerly end of Britain offers some of the country's most spectacular scenery in Britain. Land's End itself is one of the great iconic landmarks. Visited by tens of thousands annually, they come like pilgrims to this magnificent rocky point looking westward out into the Atlantic.

Inland is the ancient landscape of Penwith, heartland of Cornwall's history, teeming with the artefacts of prehistoric man, a countryside redolent of myth and legend. In more recent times mining became the dominant focus in this wild and inhospitable region, with man tunnelling far out under the sea in search of copper and tin. Today, the mining villages and fishing ports have mostly given way to tourism. But the landscape endures as the superb aerial photographs in this book portray.

Jason Hawkes is one of the country's best-known photographers specialising in aerial photography. In this book he takes the reader on a trip along the coast, looking down as seabirds do, along some of the world's most beautiful coastline.

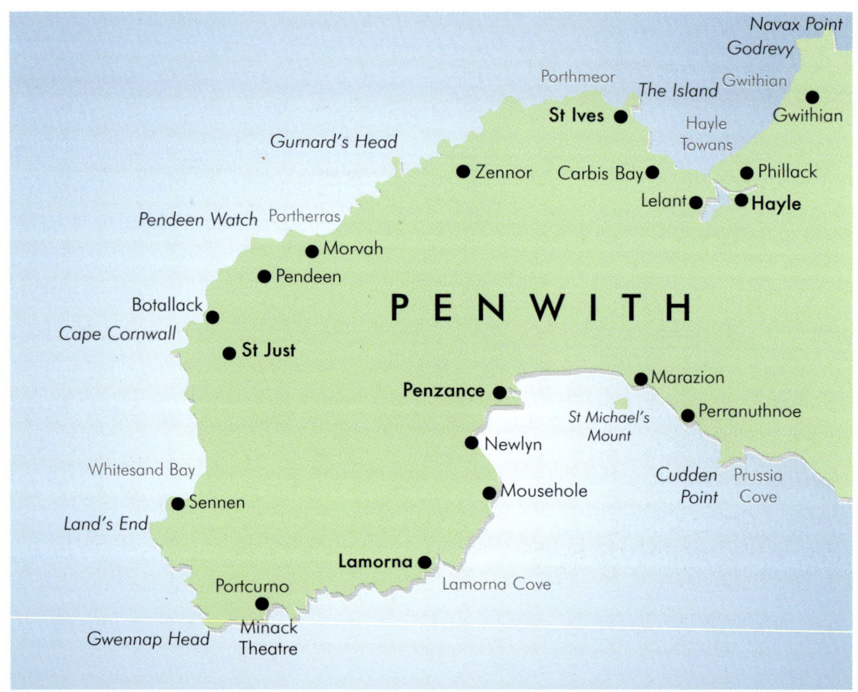
Navax Point
Godrevy
Porthmeor
The Island
Gwithian
Gwithian
St Ives
Hayle
Towans
Gurnard's Head
Zennor
Carbis Bay
Phillack
Lelant
Hayle
Pendeen Watch
Portherras
Morvah
Pendeen
PENWITH
Botallack
Cape Cornwall
St Just
Marazion
Penzance
St Michael's
Mount
Perranuthnoe
Newlyn
Whitesand Bay
Cudden
Point
Prussia
Cove
Mousehole
Sennen
Land's End
Lamorna
Lamorna Cove
Portcurno
Minack
Theatre
Gwennap Head

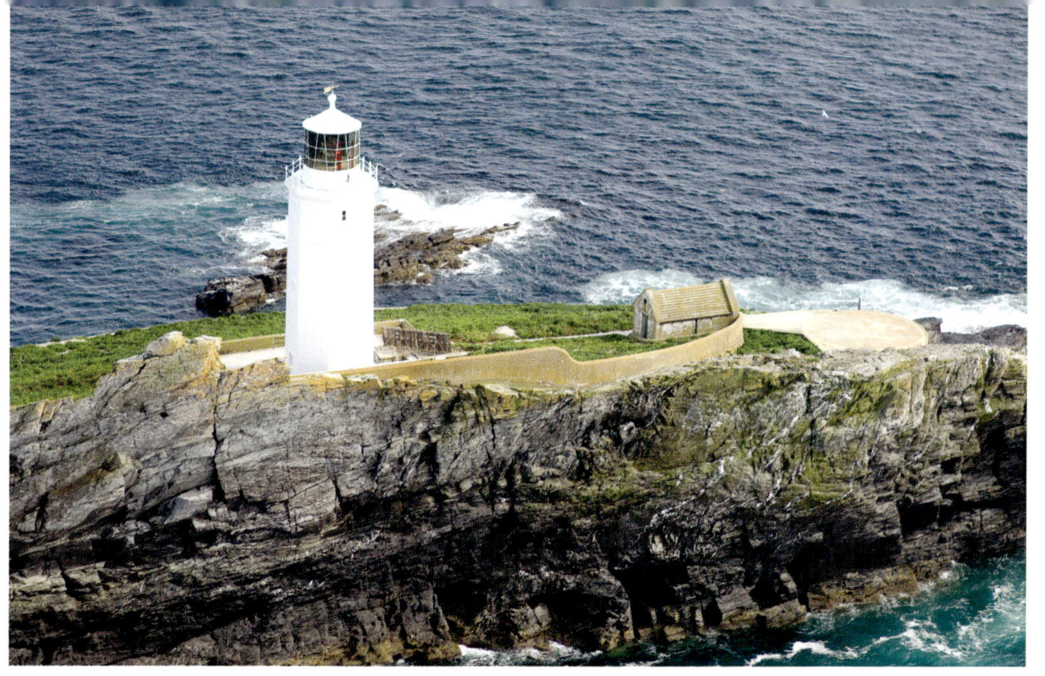

Godrevy lighthouse guards the eastern side of St Ives Bay and marks the boundary, so some would say, of the region known as Penwith.

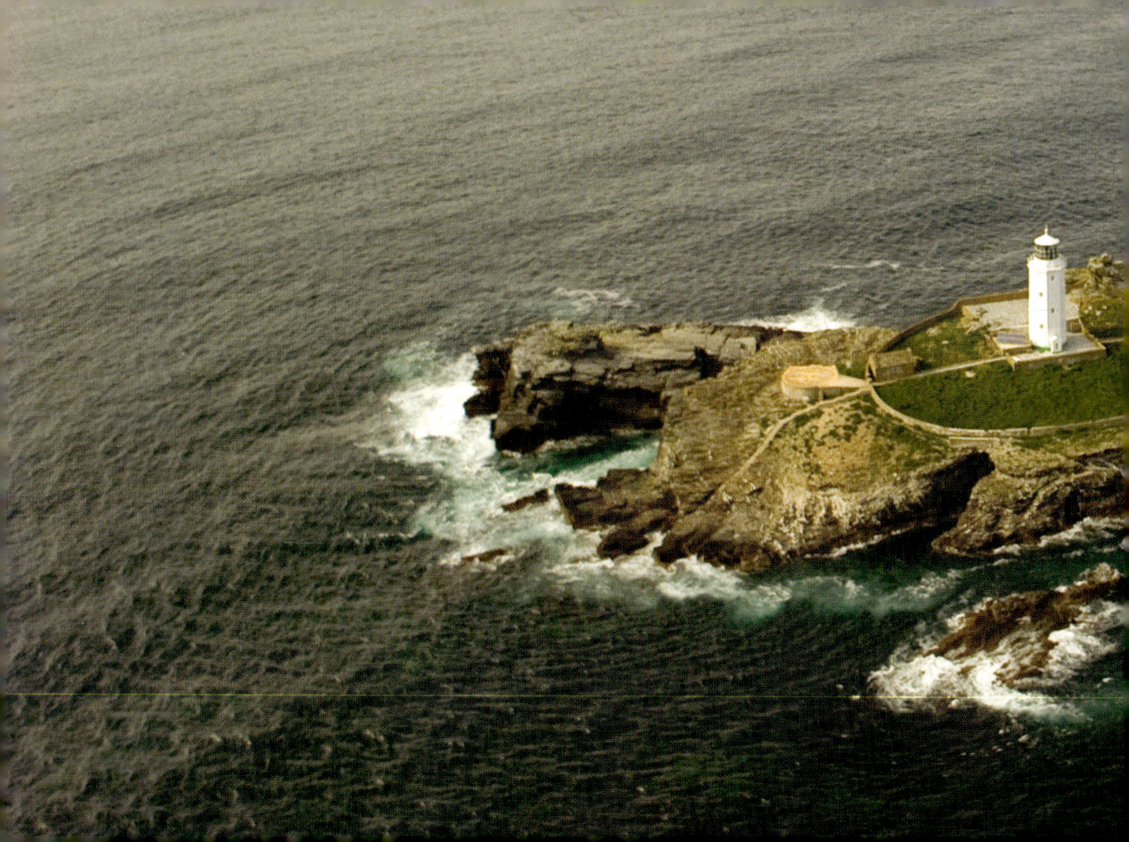

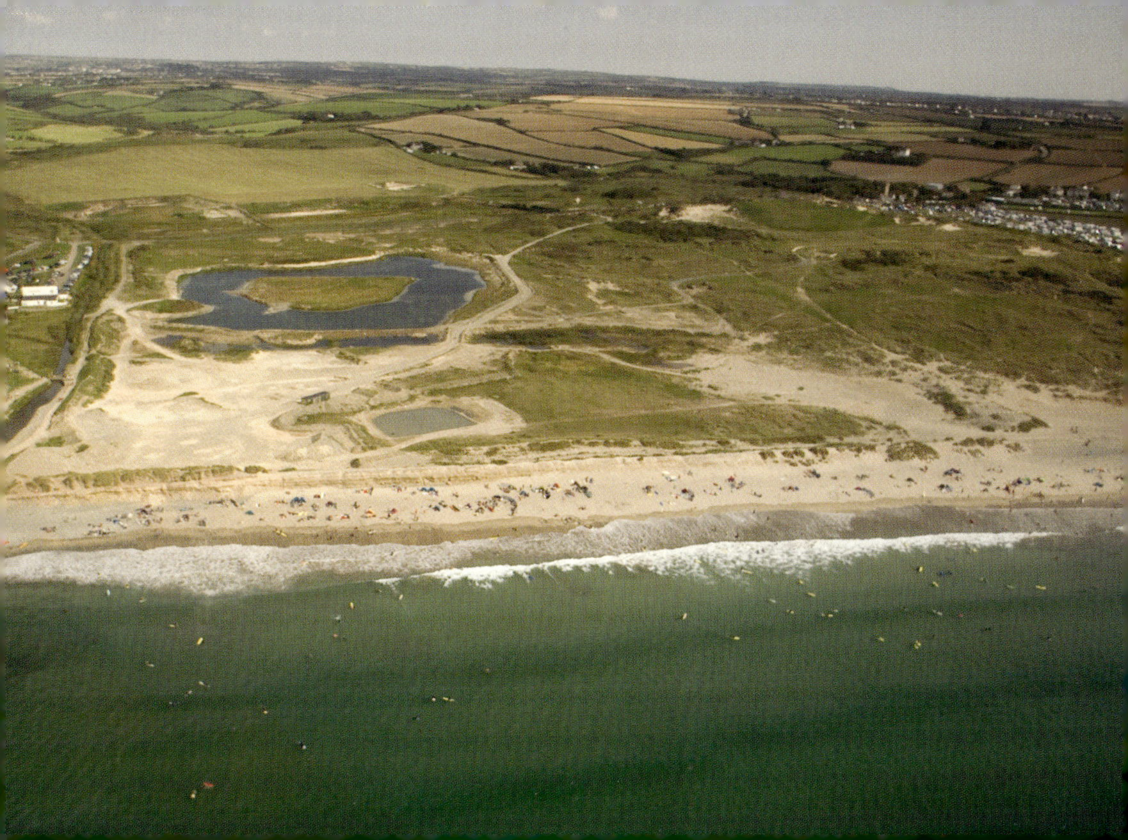

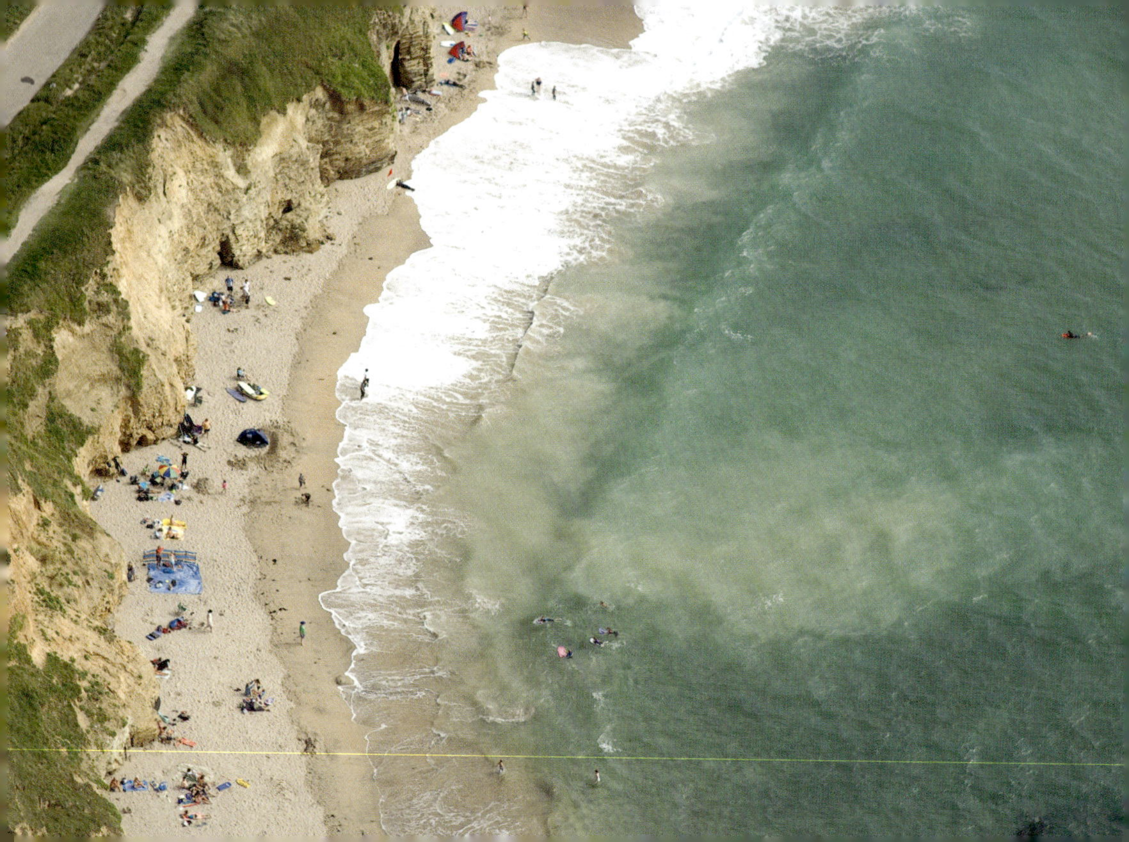

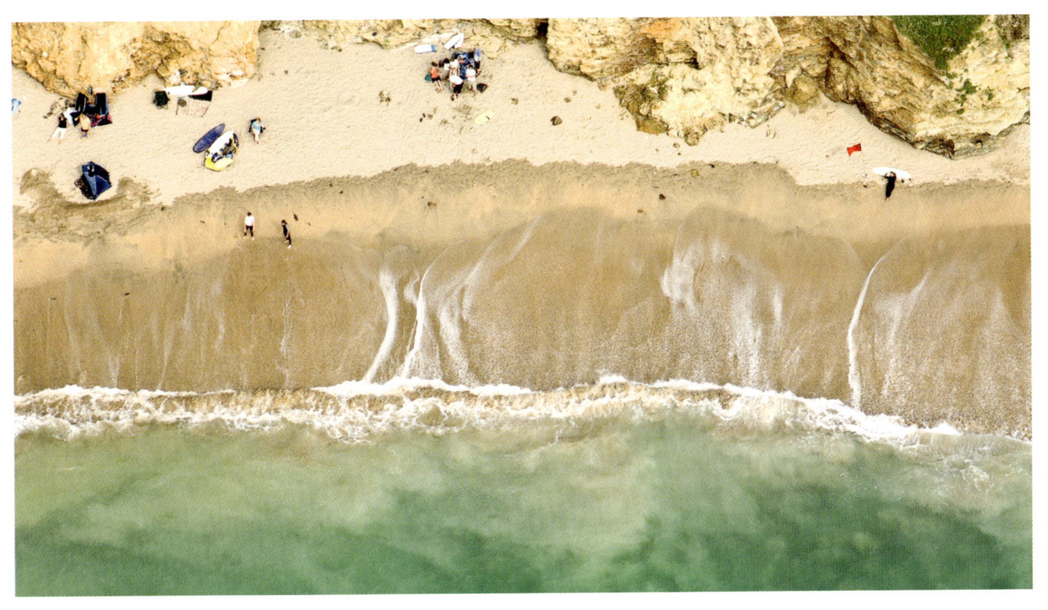

Left and above: Holidaymakers retreat before the rising tide at Upton Towans beach, just east of Hayle.

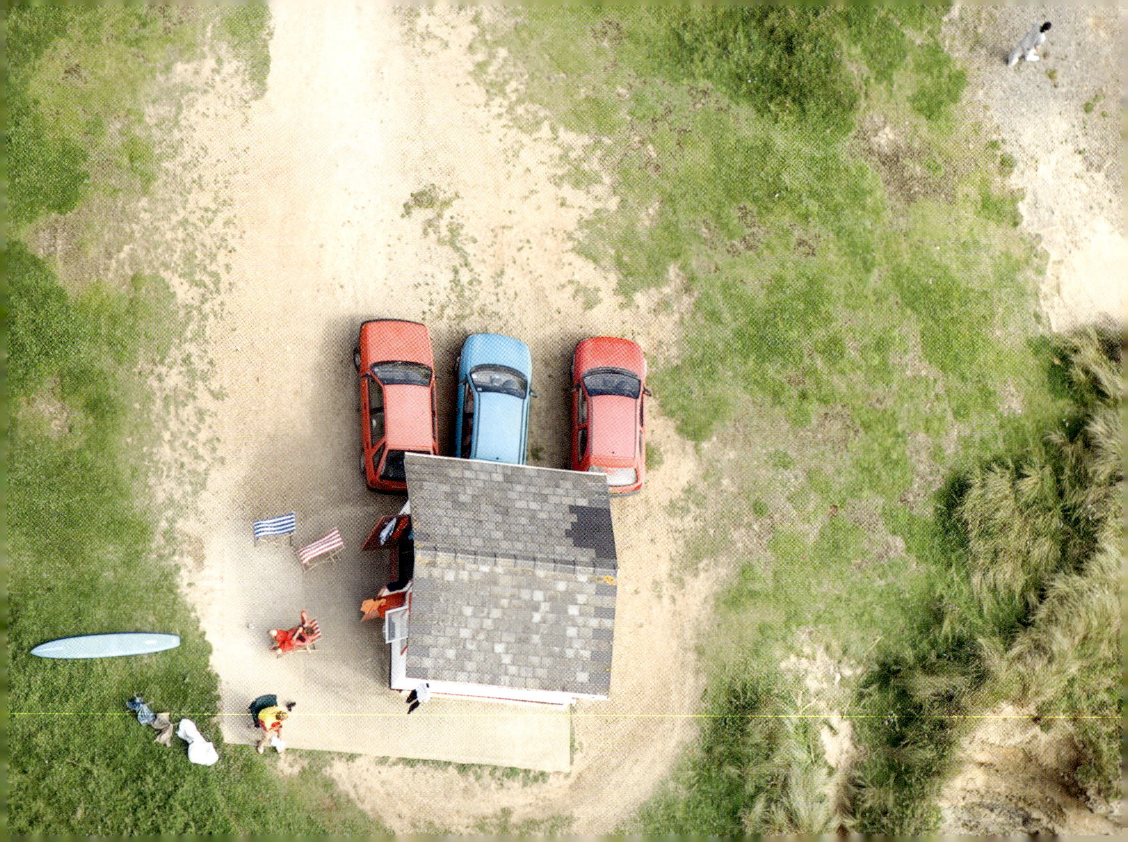

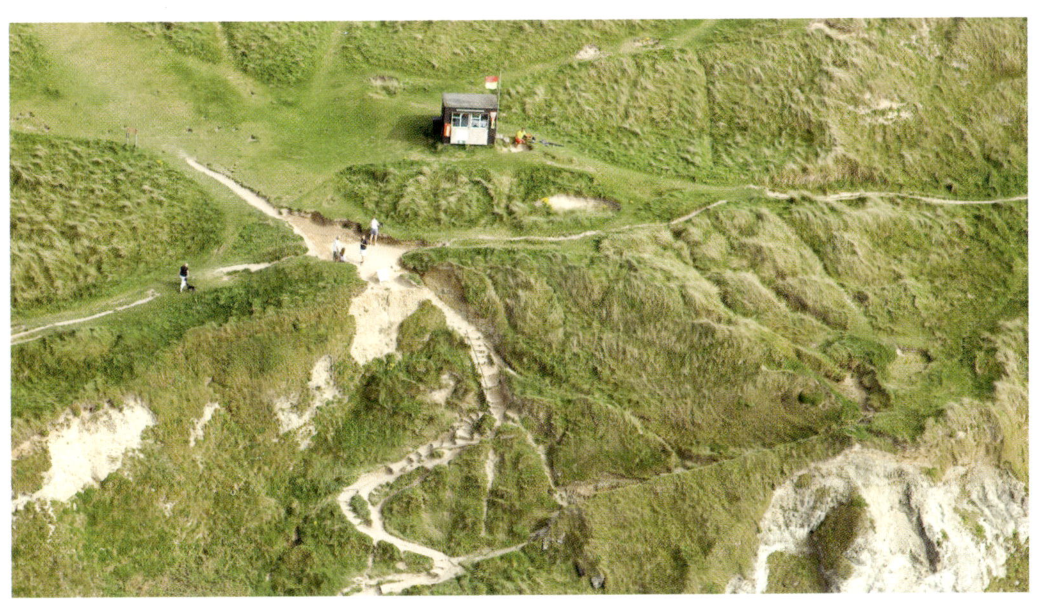

Left and above: A beach hut and a lifeguard station overlooks the beach near Gwithian.

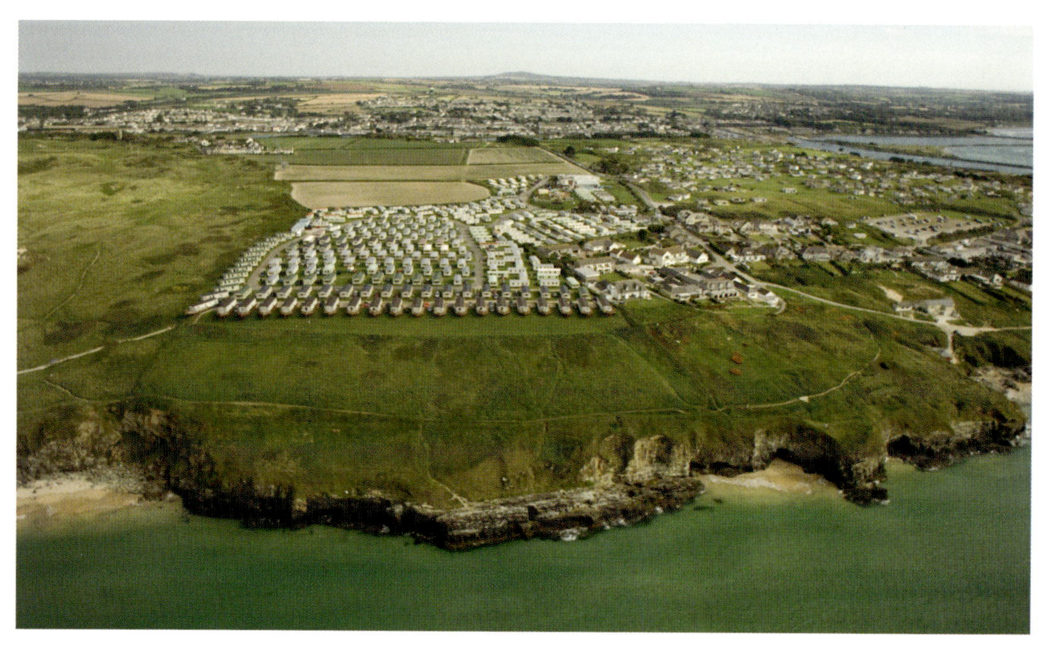

Above and right: Static caravans lined up neatly at The Towans holiday camp, with (right) the view into Hayle.

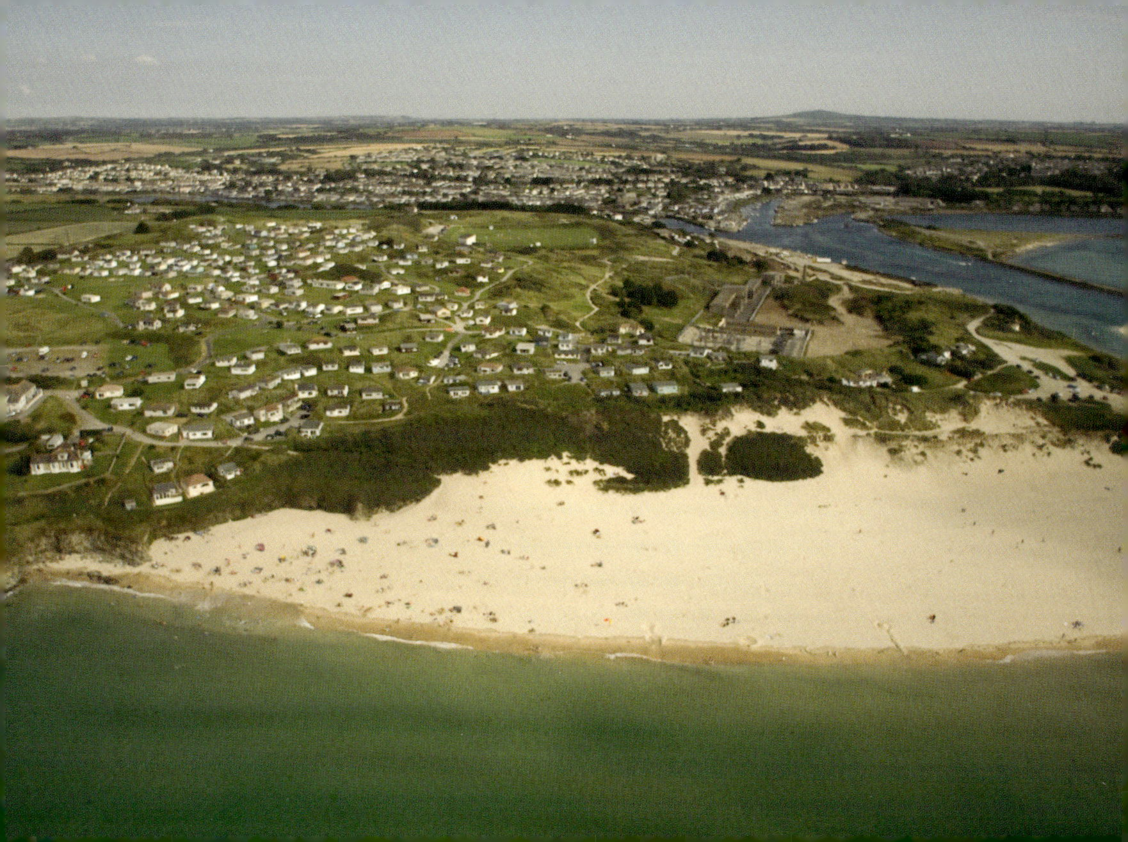

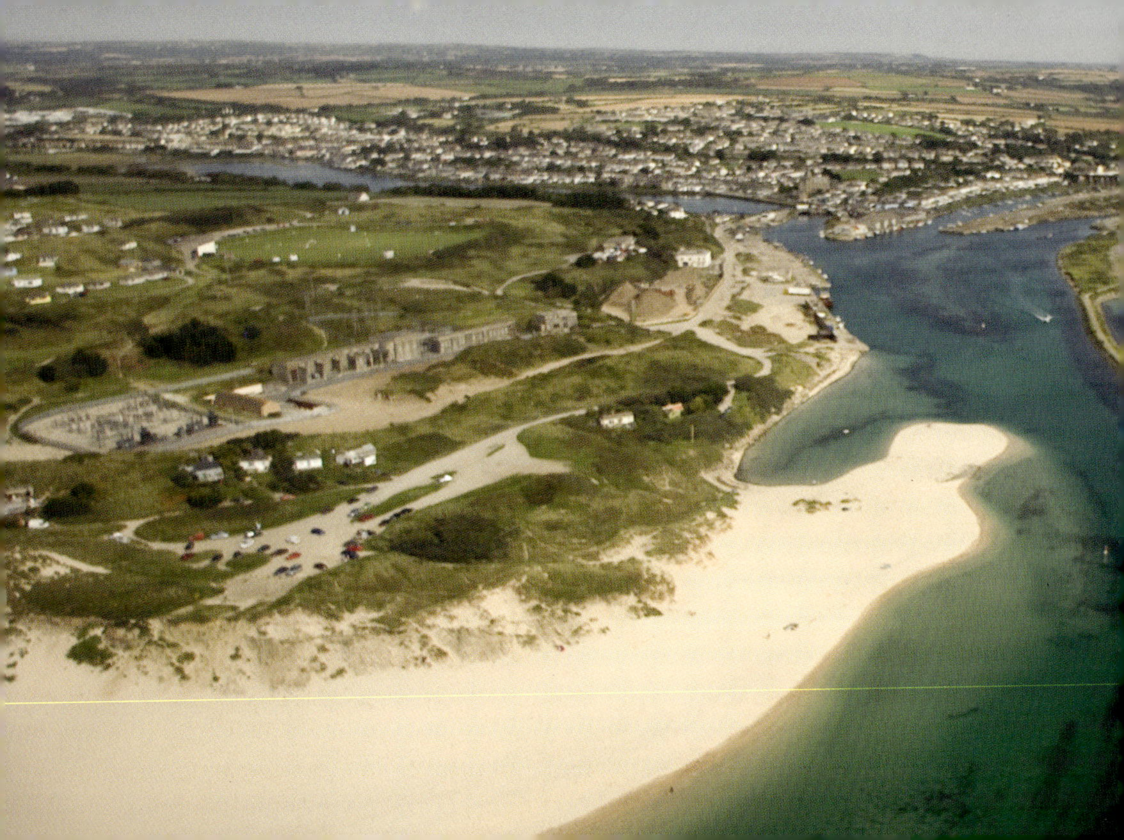

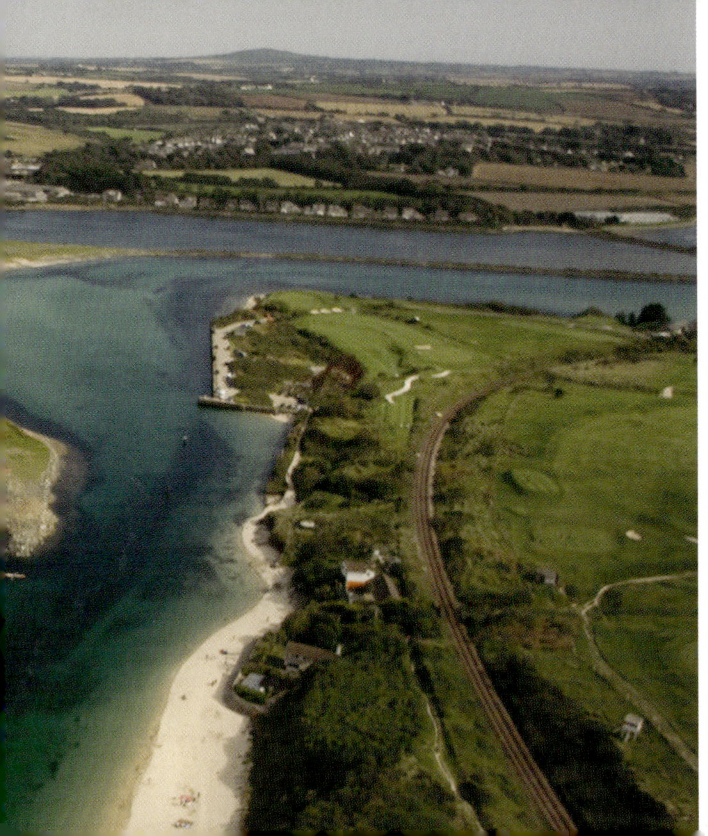

Hayle, was once a busy harbour servicing foundries and manufacturing industries associated with mining. It is now largely reliant on tourism.

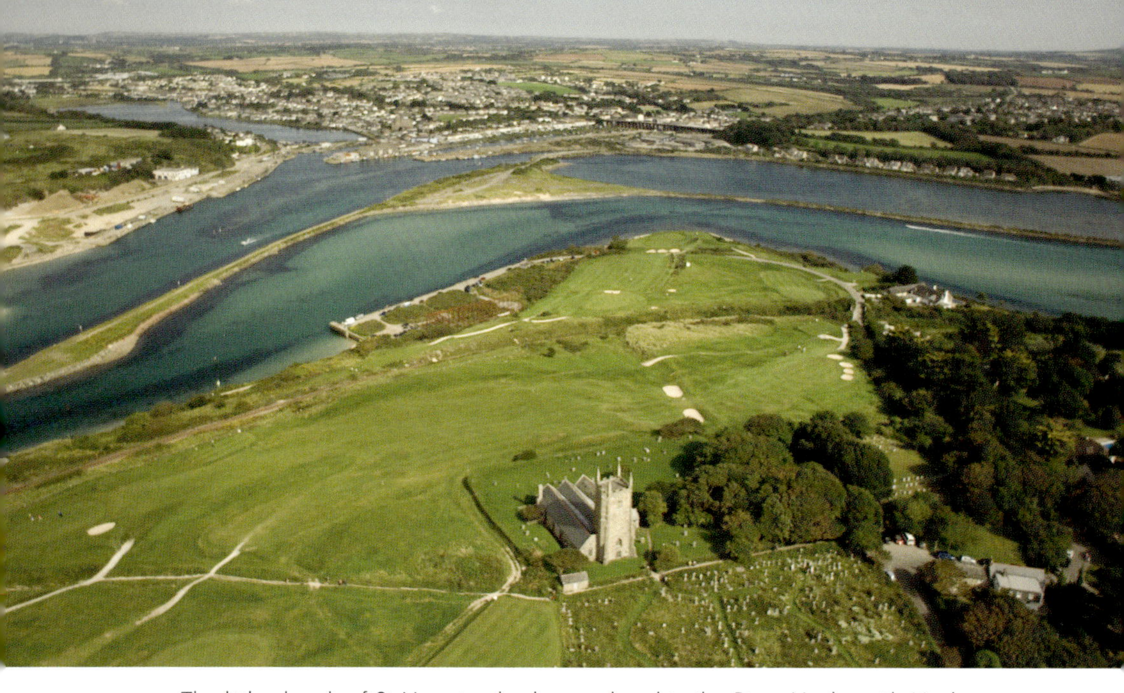

The little church of St Uny stands above a bend in the River Hayle, with Hayle in the middle distance.

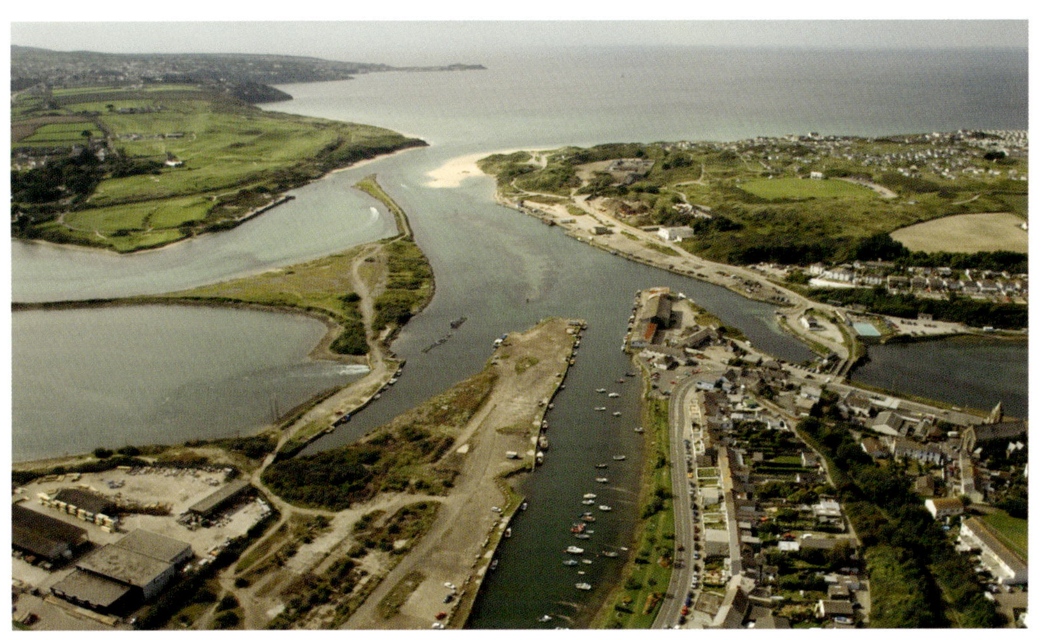

Looking out to sea from Hayle.

A glimpse of the Summer Game; cricket at St Ives.

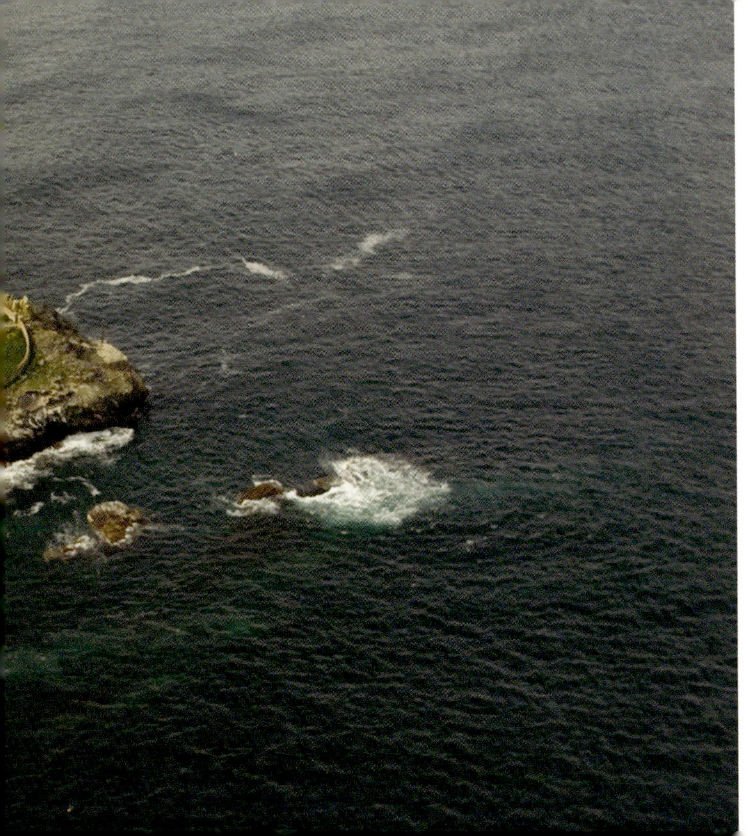

Godrevy Lighthouse.

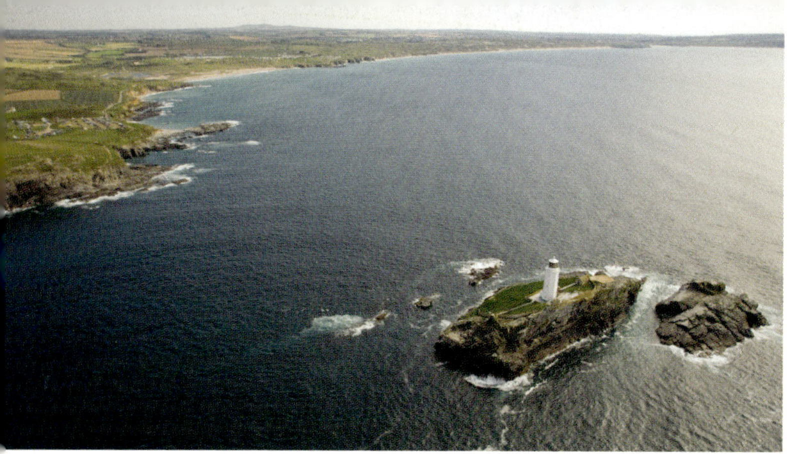

A spectacular view south-westwards across Godrevy Island taking in the whole of St Ives Bay, with the sand dunes known as The Towans at the entrance into Hayle and Carbis Bay.

Opposite:
Looking inland over The Towans with the village of Gwithian on the right. The Red River (its waters coloured by mineworks in the past) runs into the sea on the left.

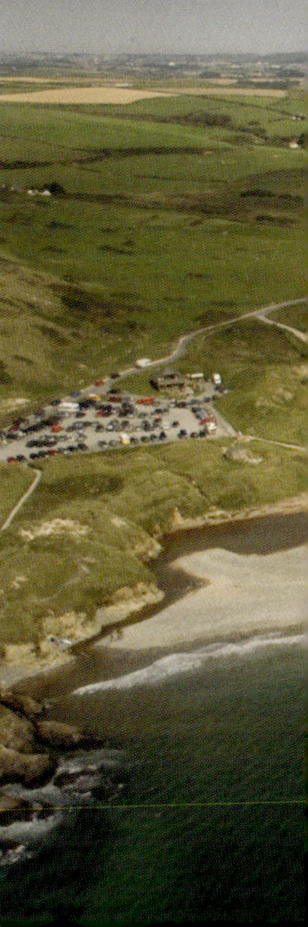

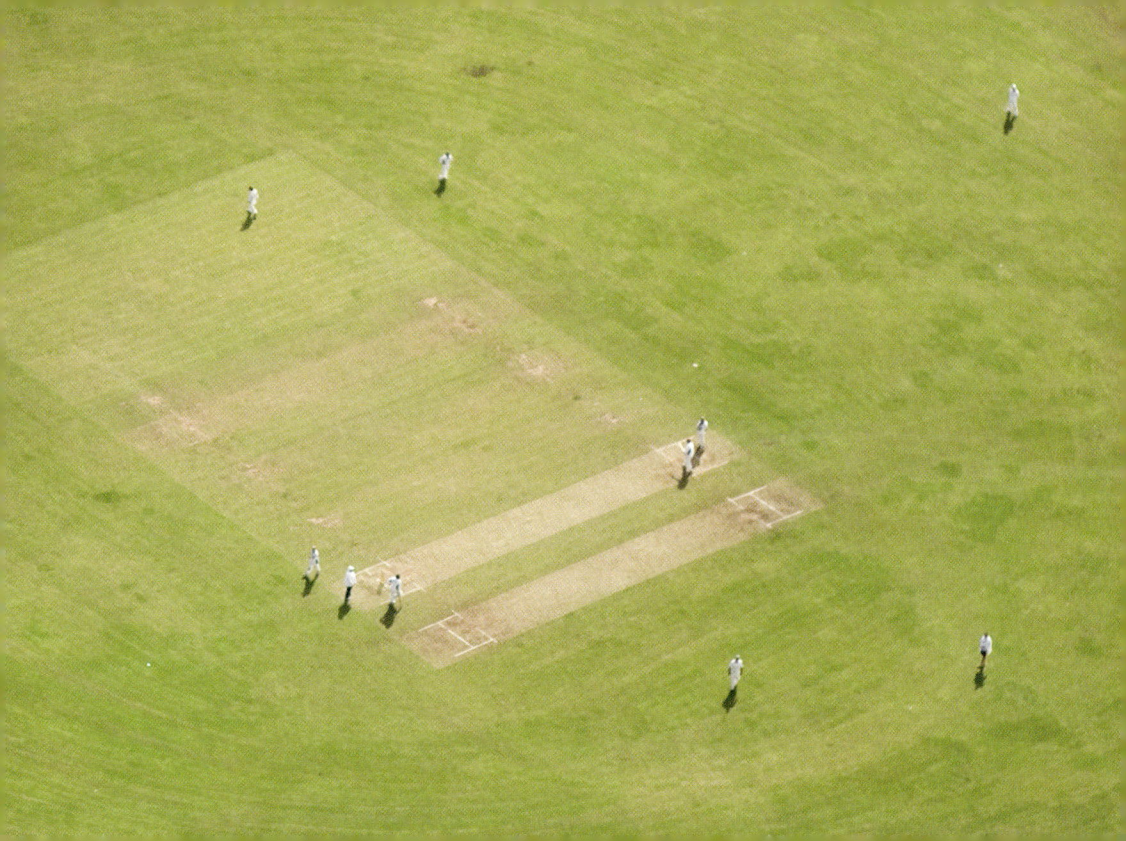

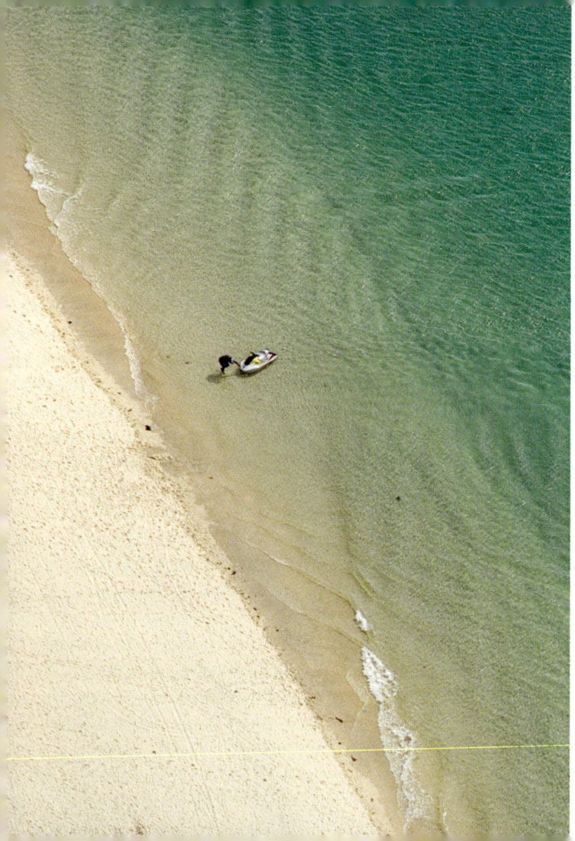

The clear green sea in Carbis Bay has a Caribbean look.

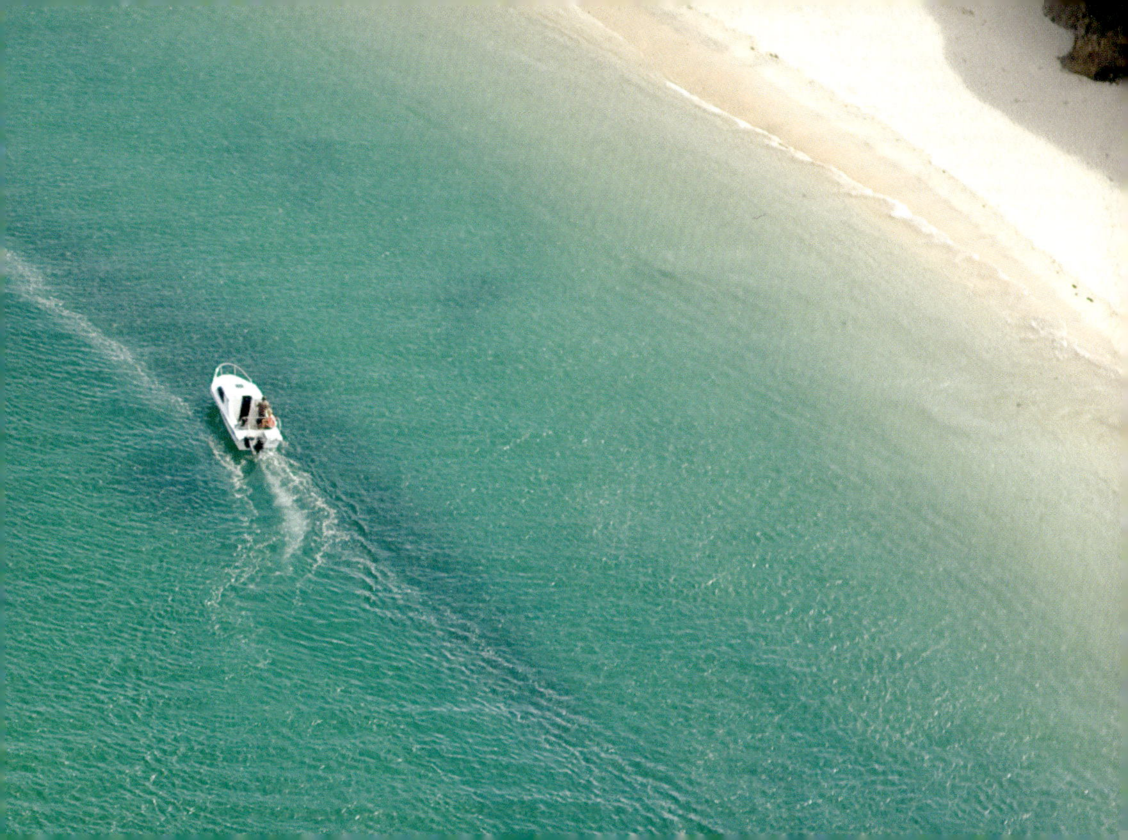

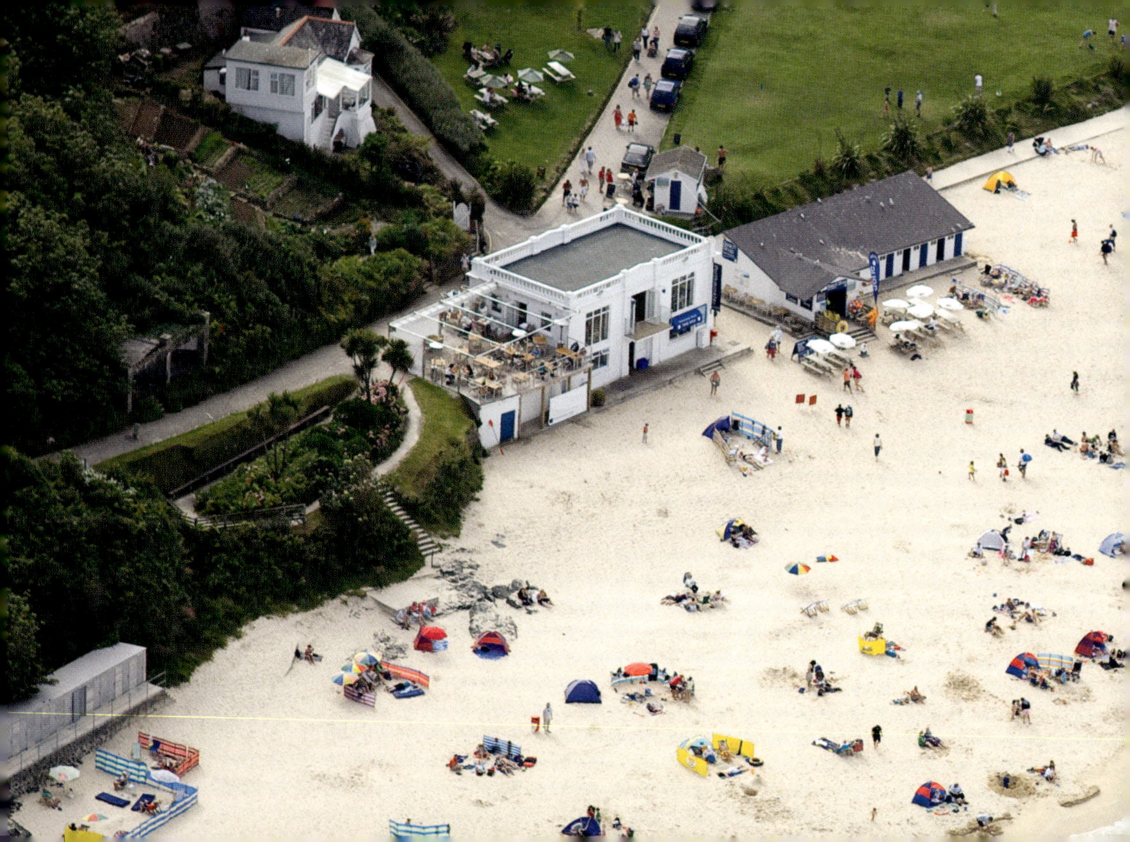

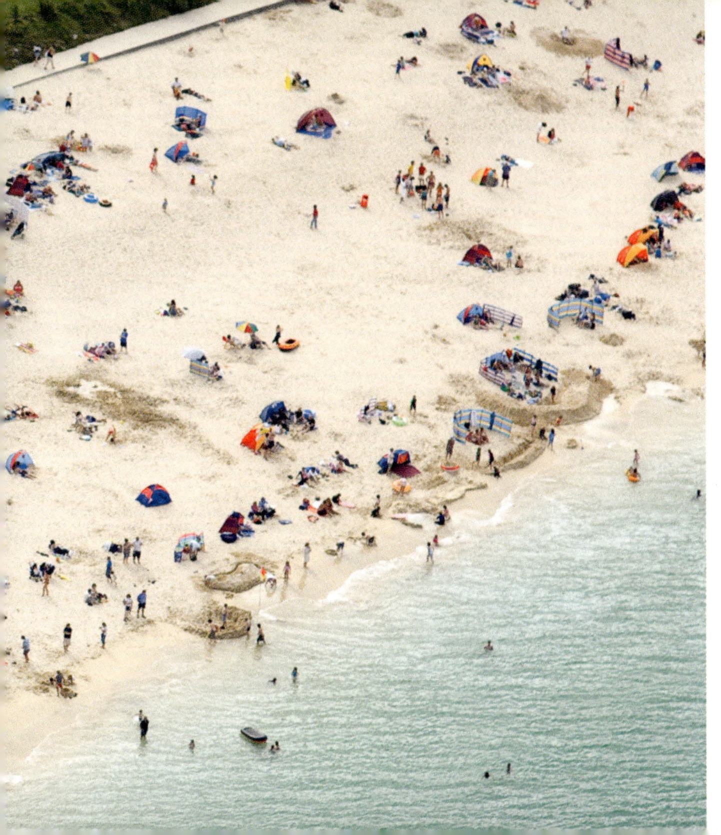

Packed sands alongside the celebrated beach café at Porthminster, St Ives.

St Ia's church, the saint from whom St Ives takes its name, dominates the centre of the town.

Overleaf:
High tide in the harbour at St Ives.

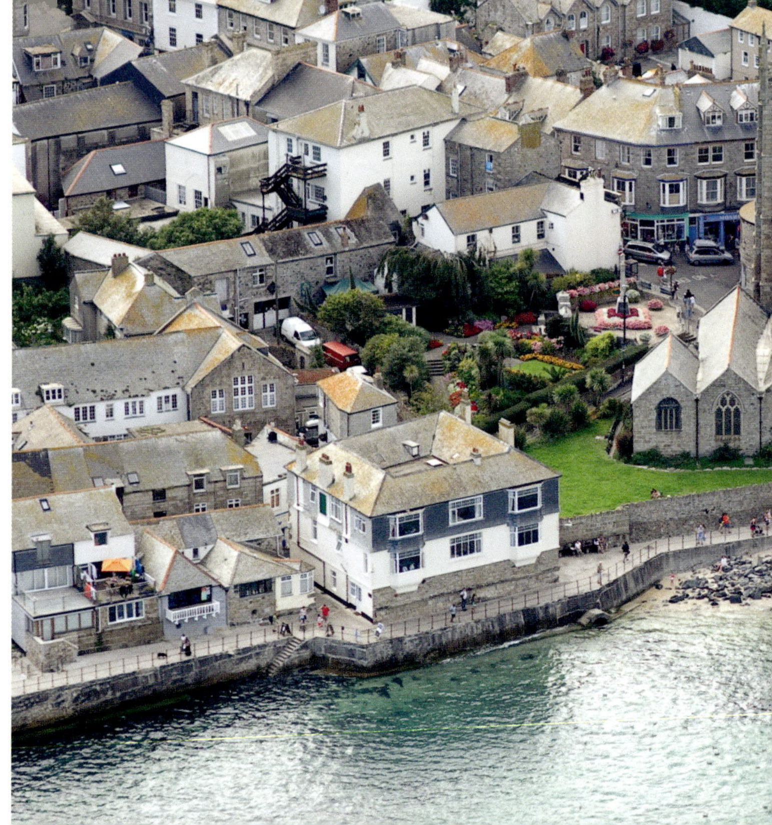

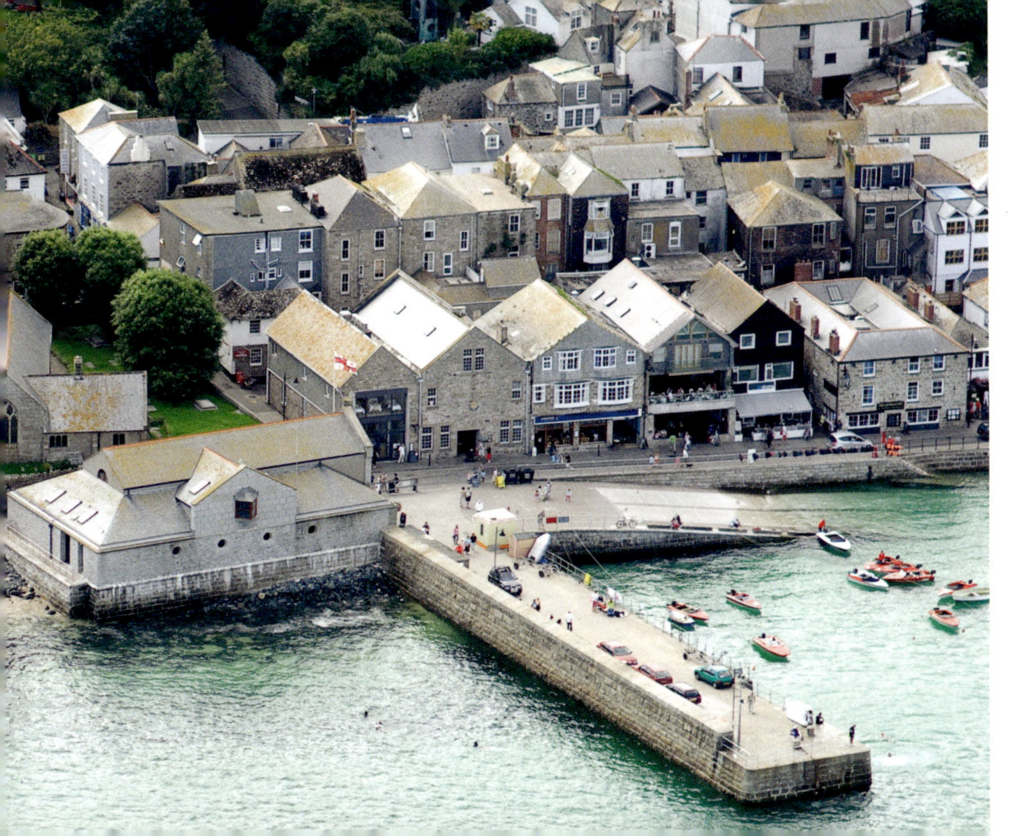

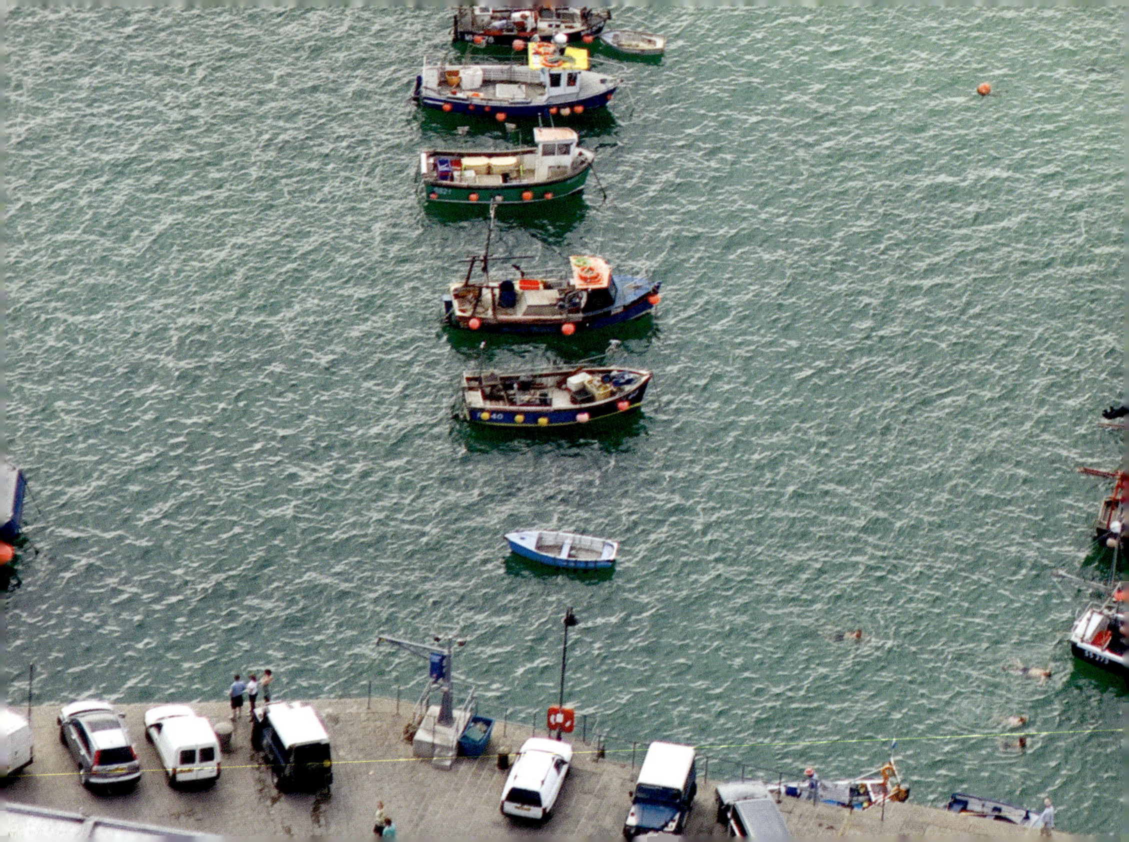

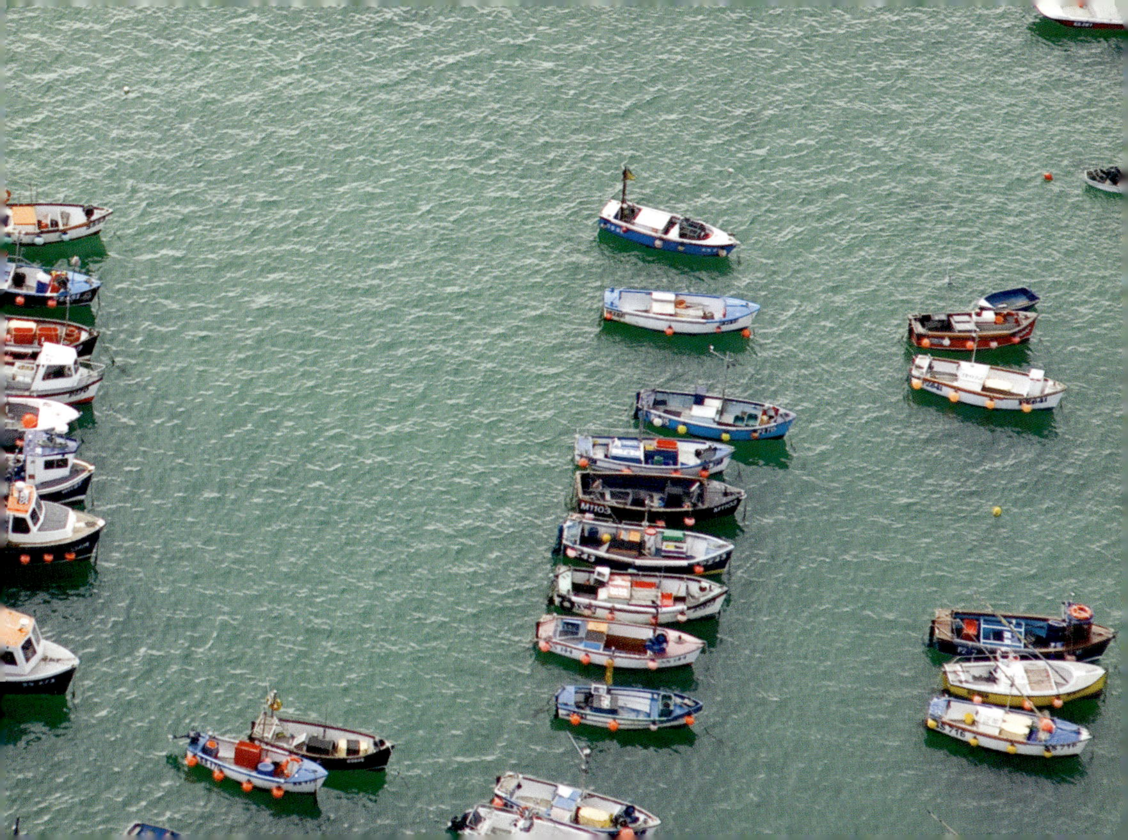

Quay Street, St Ives, always seems busy, but is especially so in summer.

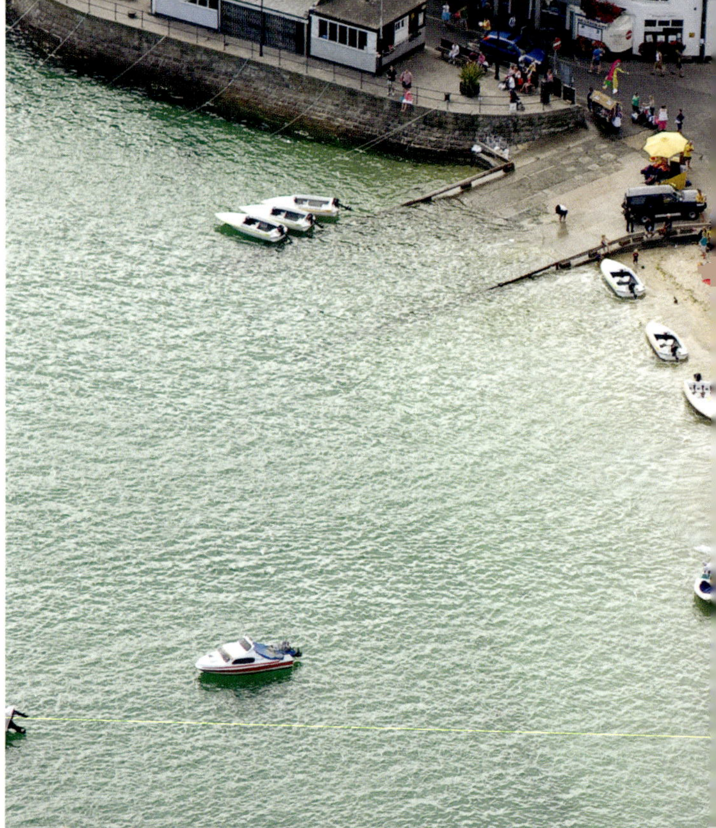

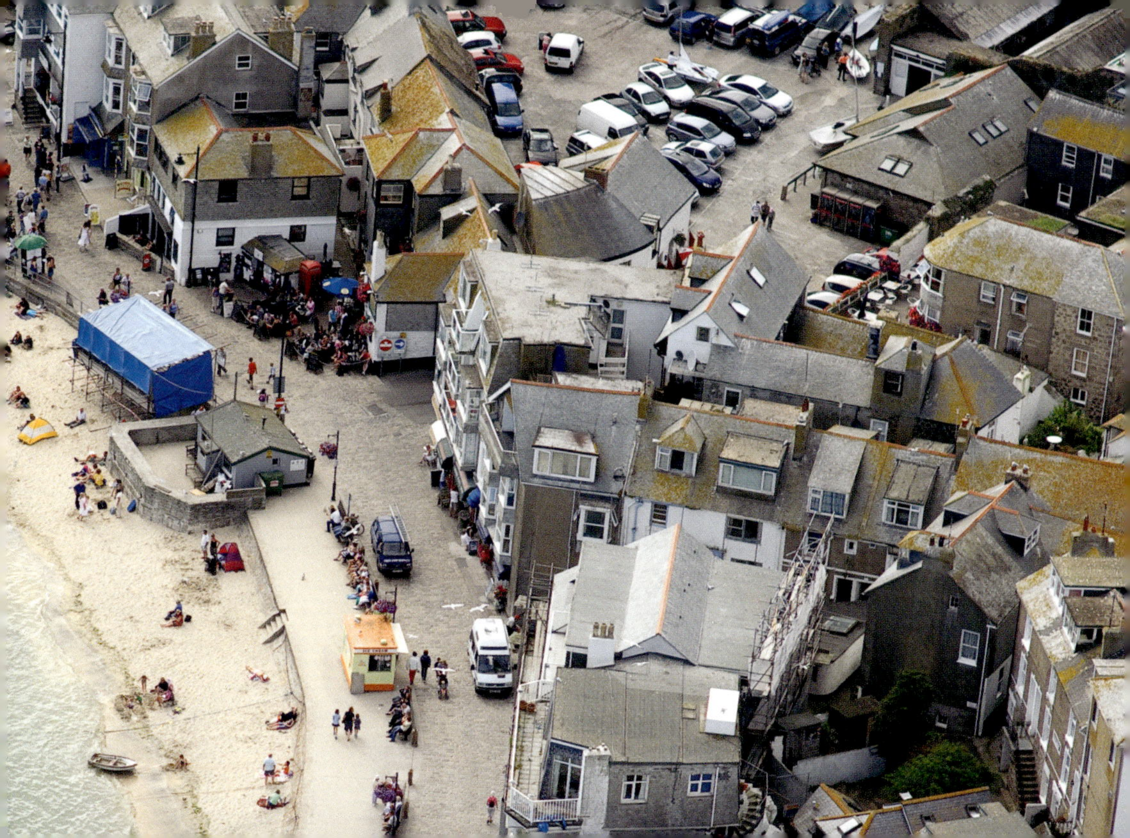

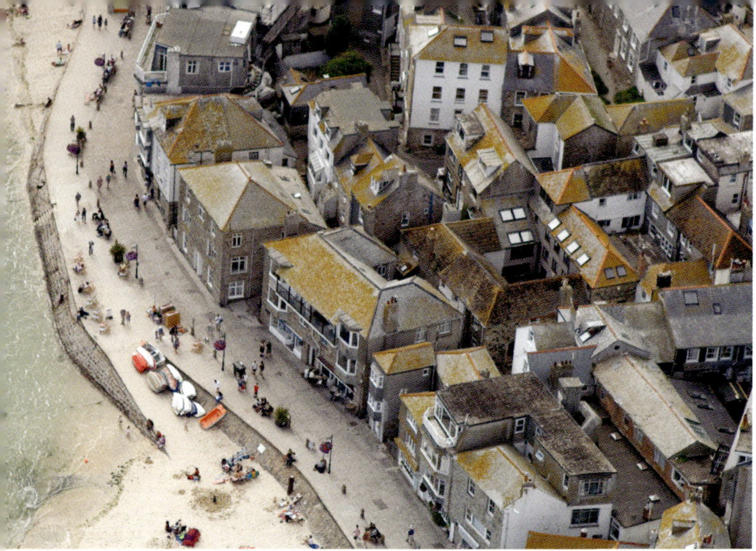

St Ives: looking down on
Quay Street and Back Road East.

Opposite:
A spectacular view out over The Island, with the harbour on the right and Tate St Ives overlooking Porthmeor Beach.

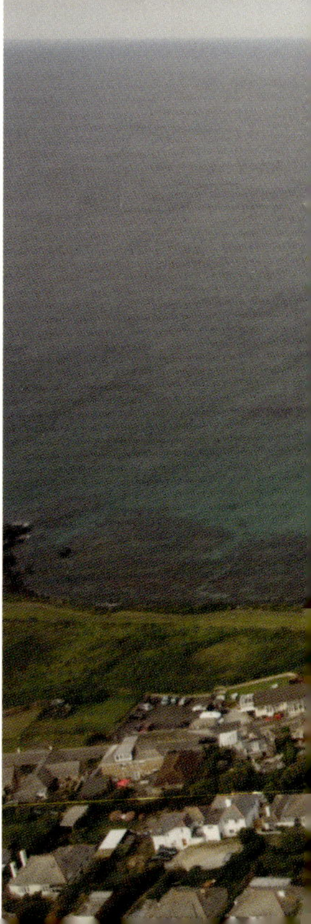

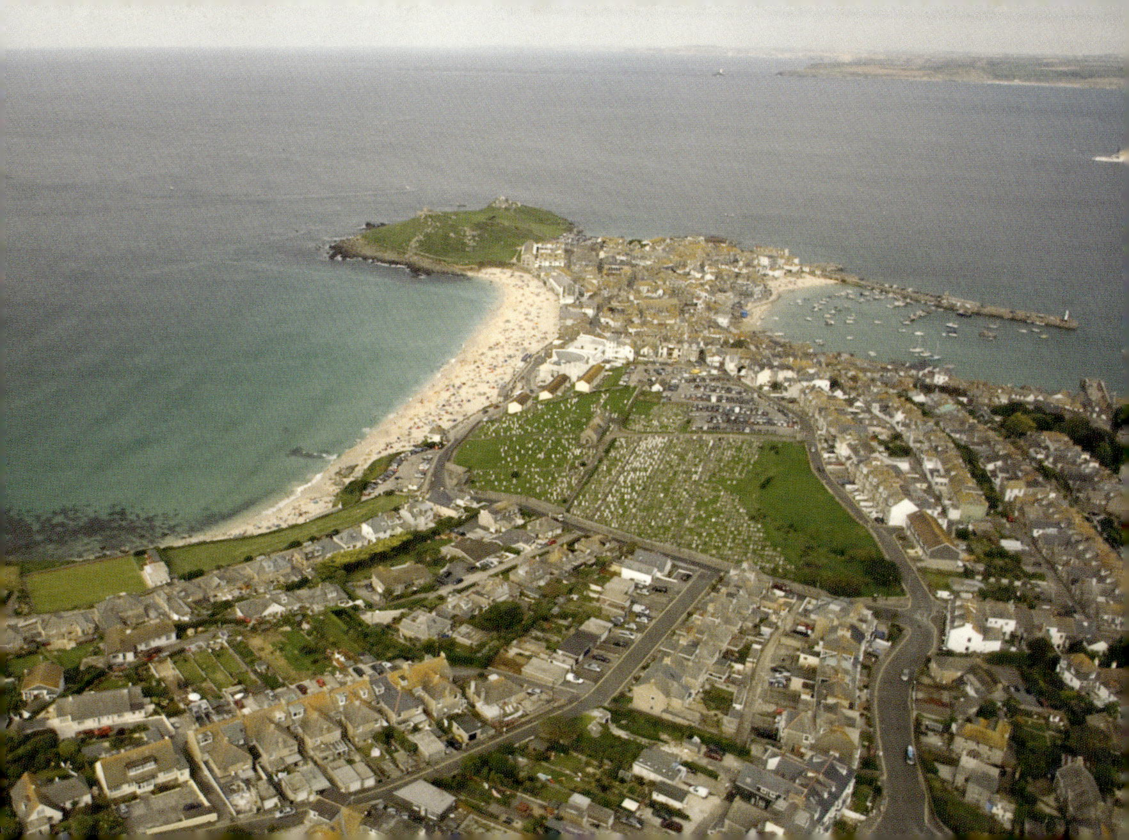

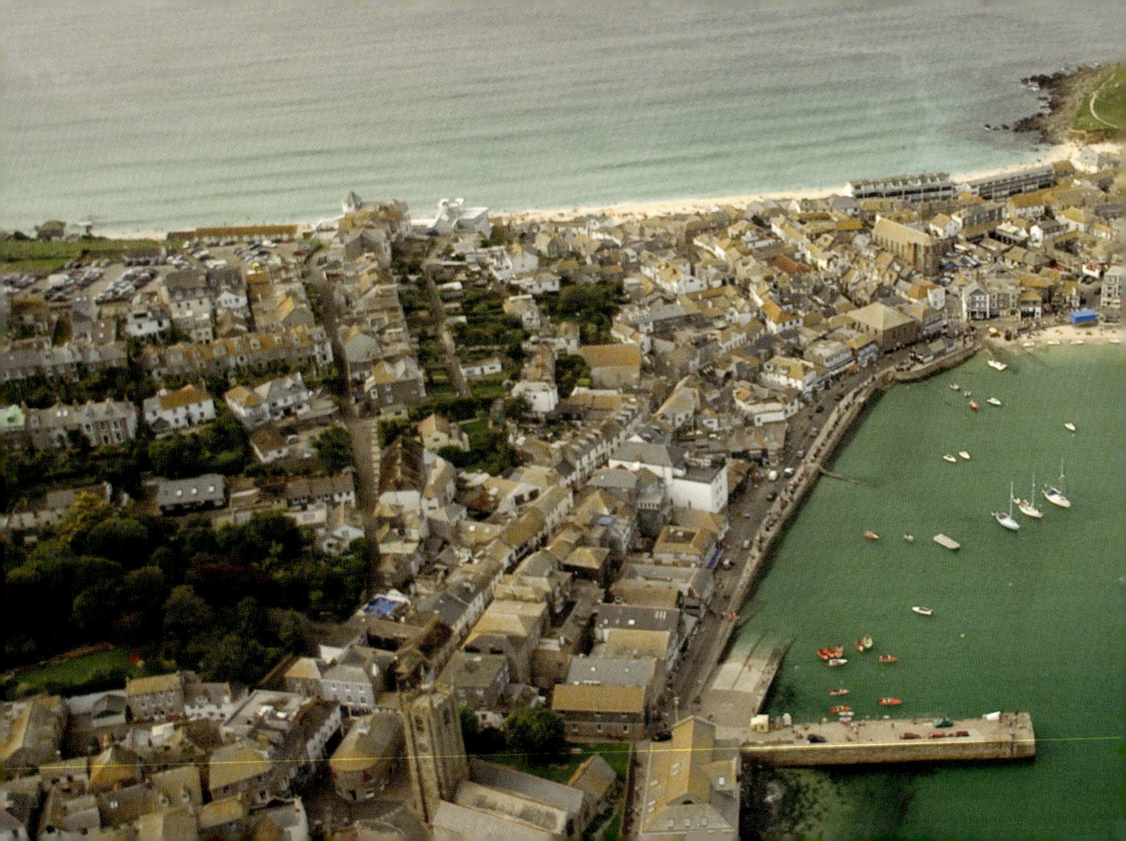

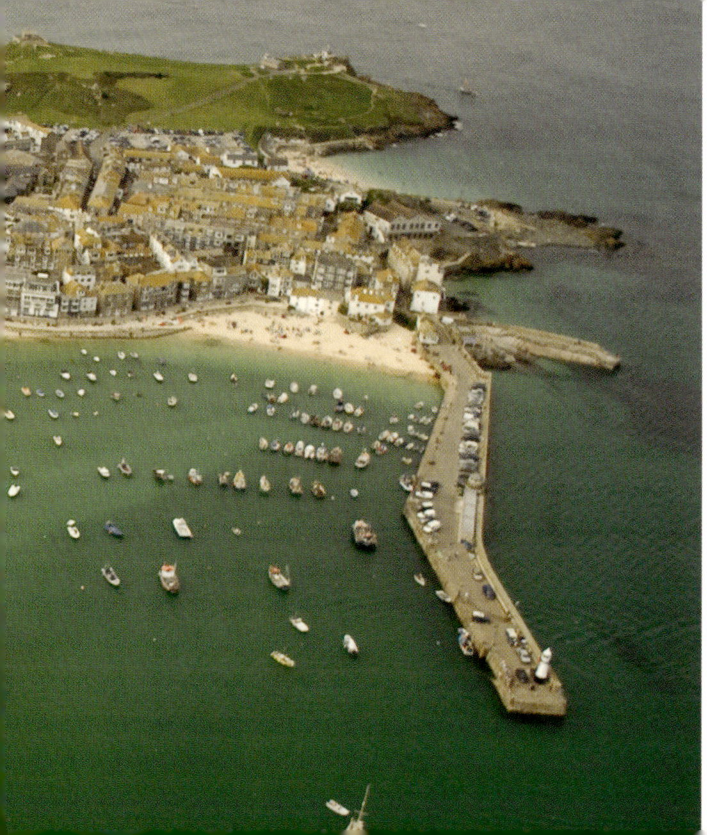

St Ives town and harbour.

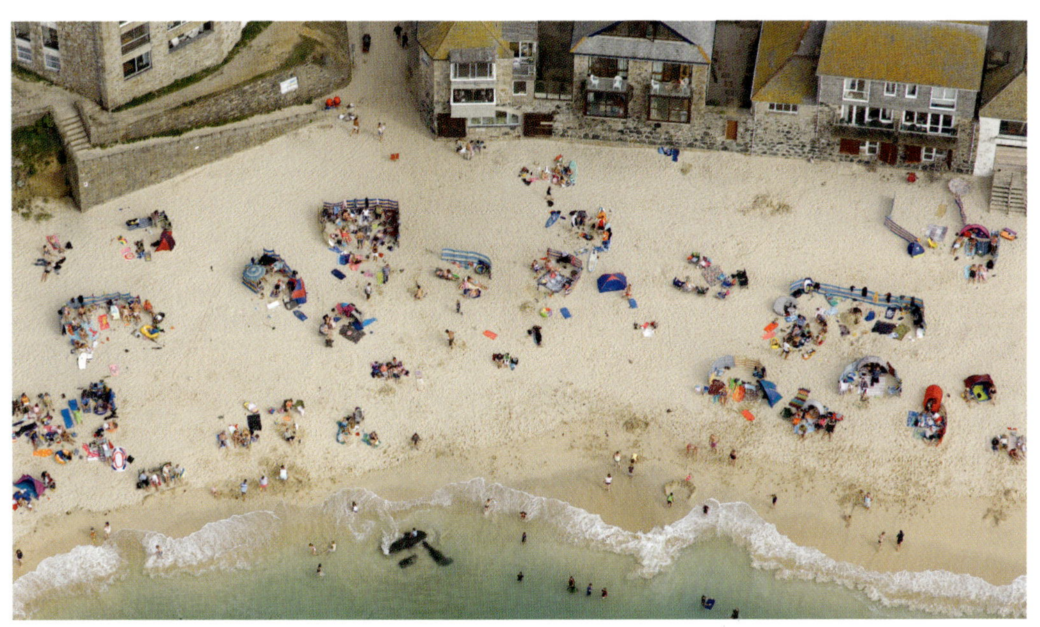

Porthmeor Beach. The former fishlofts crowding the shore have housed studios of many famous artists.

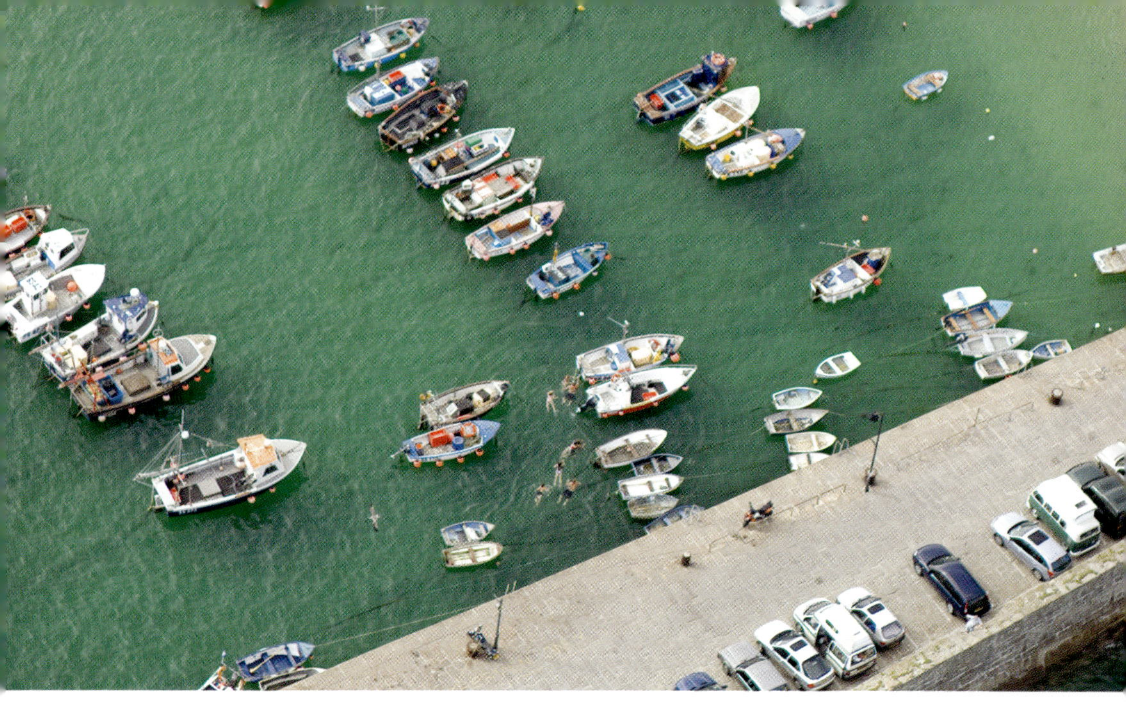

A seagull's eye view of the harbour and Smeaton's pier, St Ives.

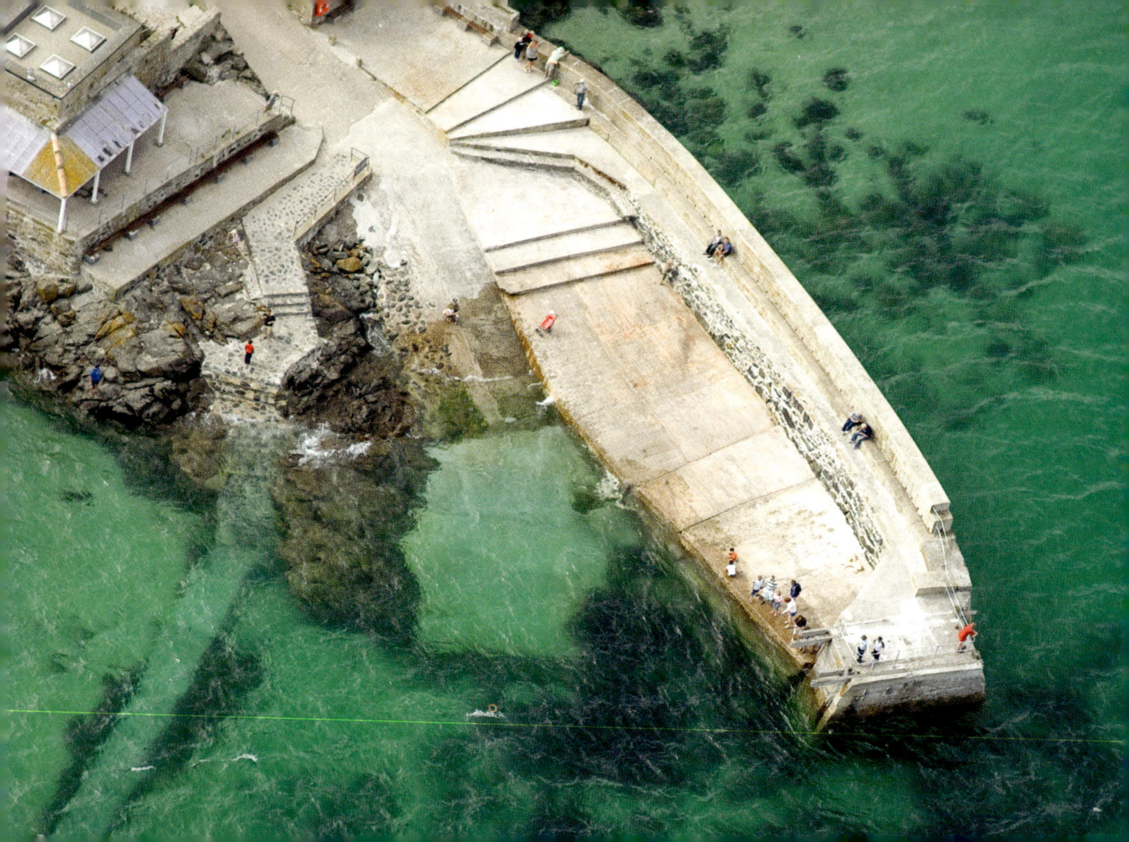

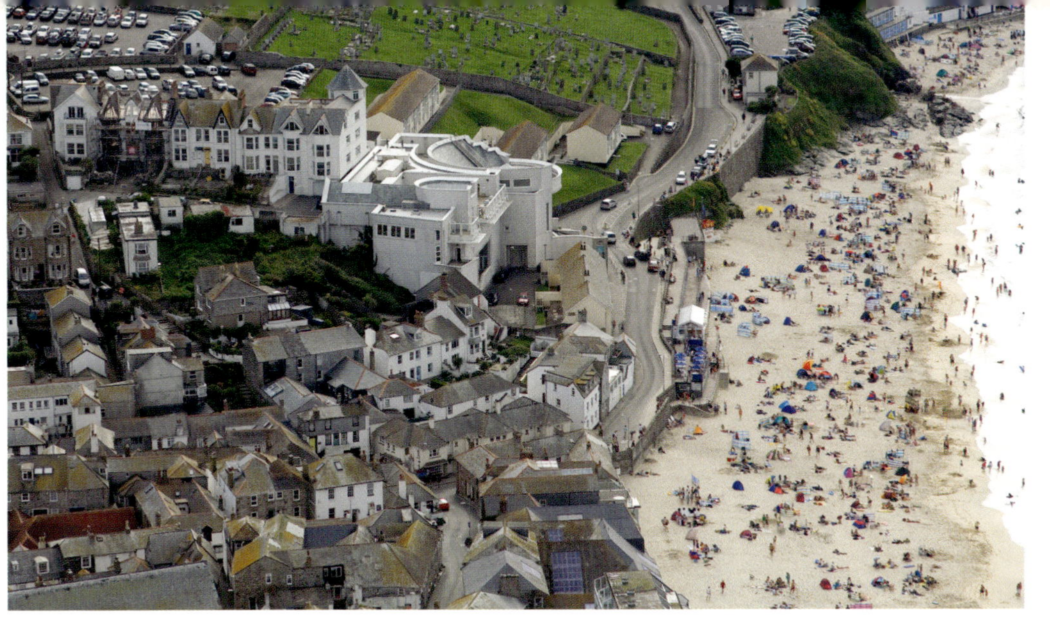

Tate St Ives and Porthmeor Beach.

Opposite:
Harbour wall, St Ives.

Looking across the ancient landscape of West Penwith, near Zennor.

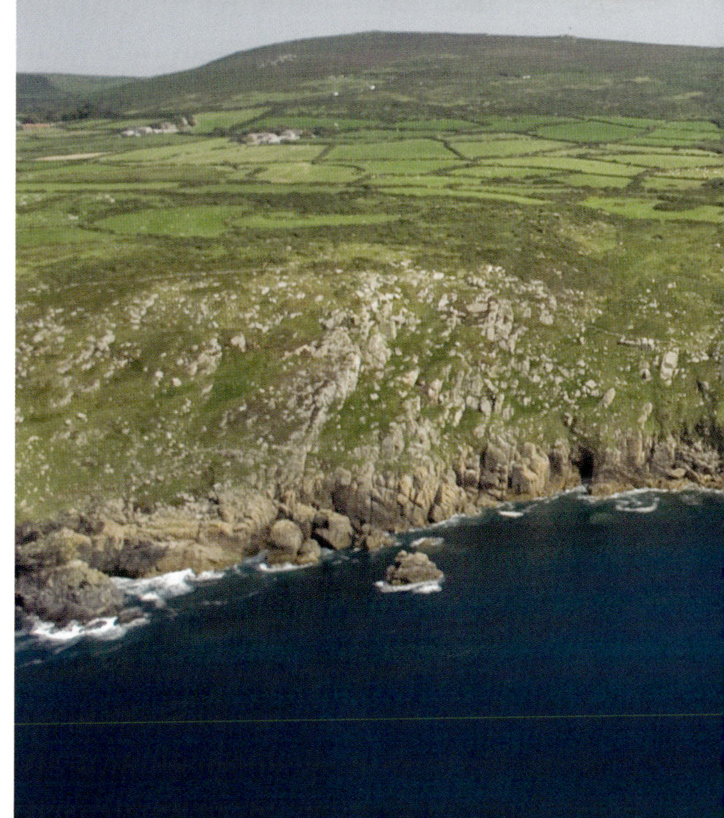

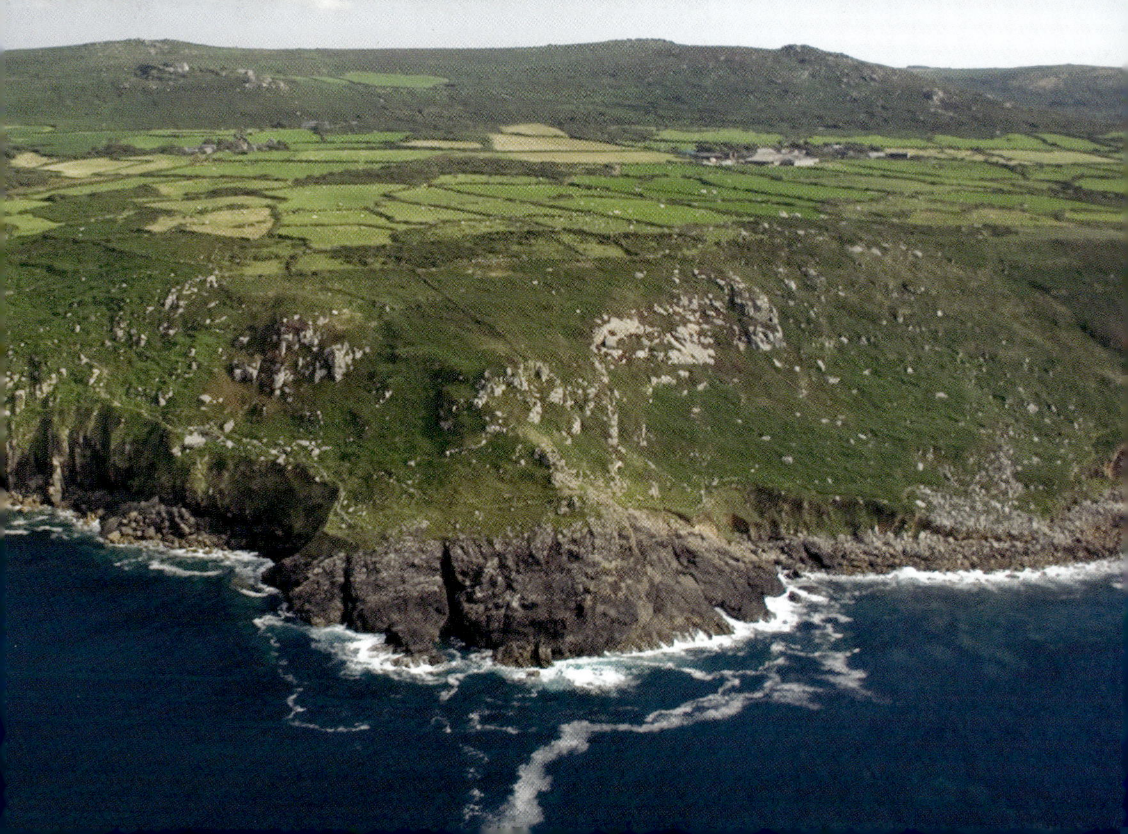

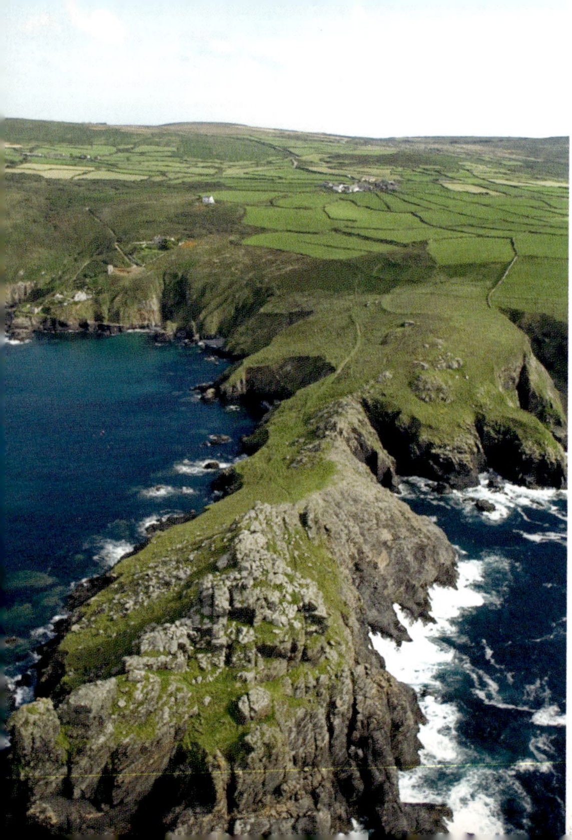

Gurnard's Head.

Right:
Looking east across Gurnard's Head over West Penwith.

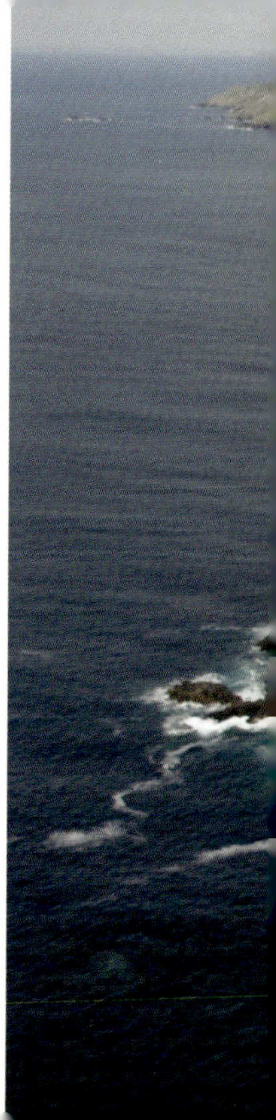

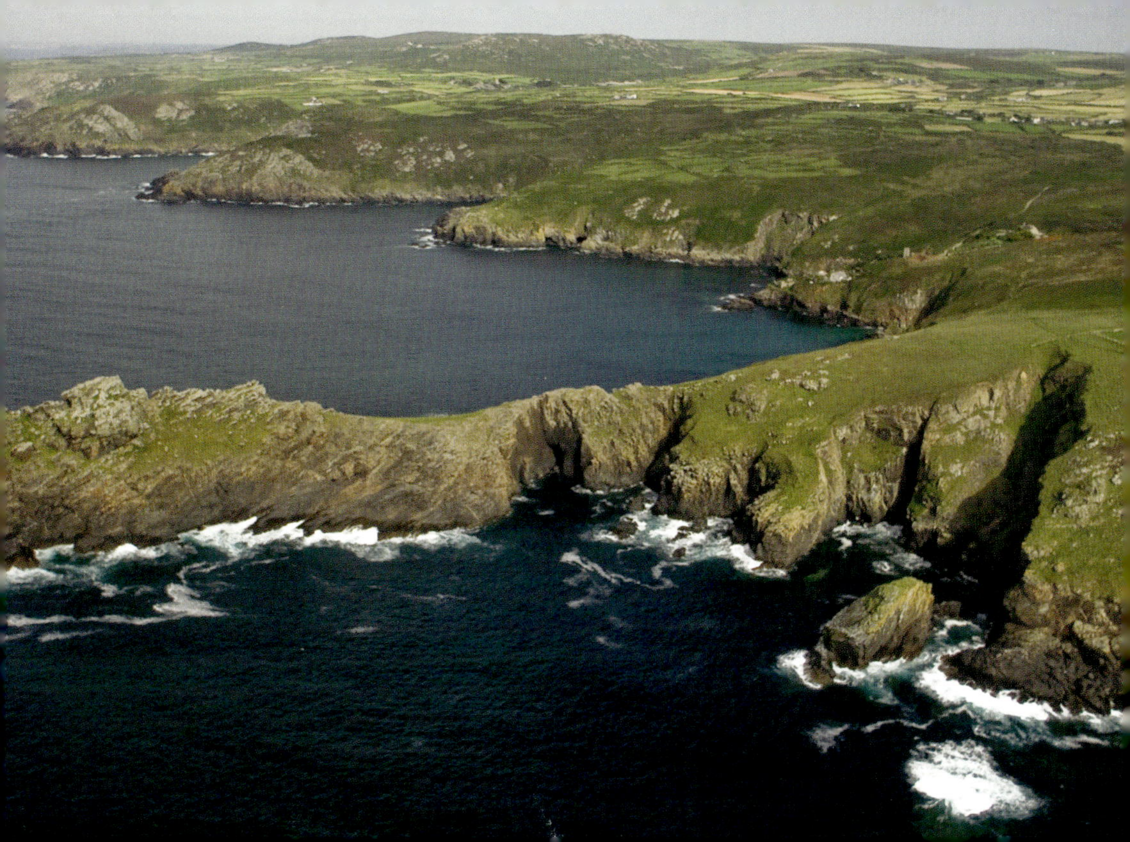

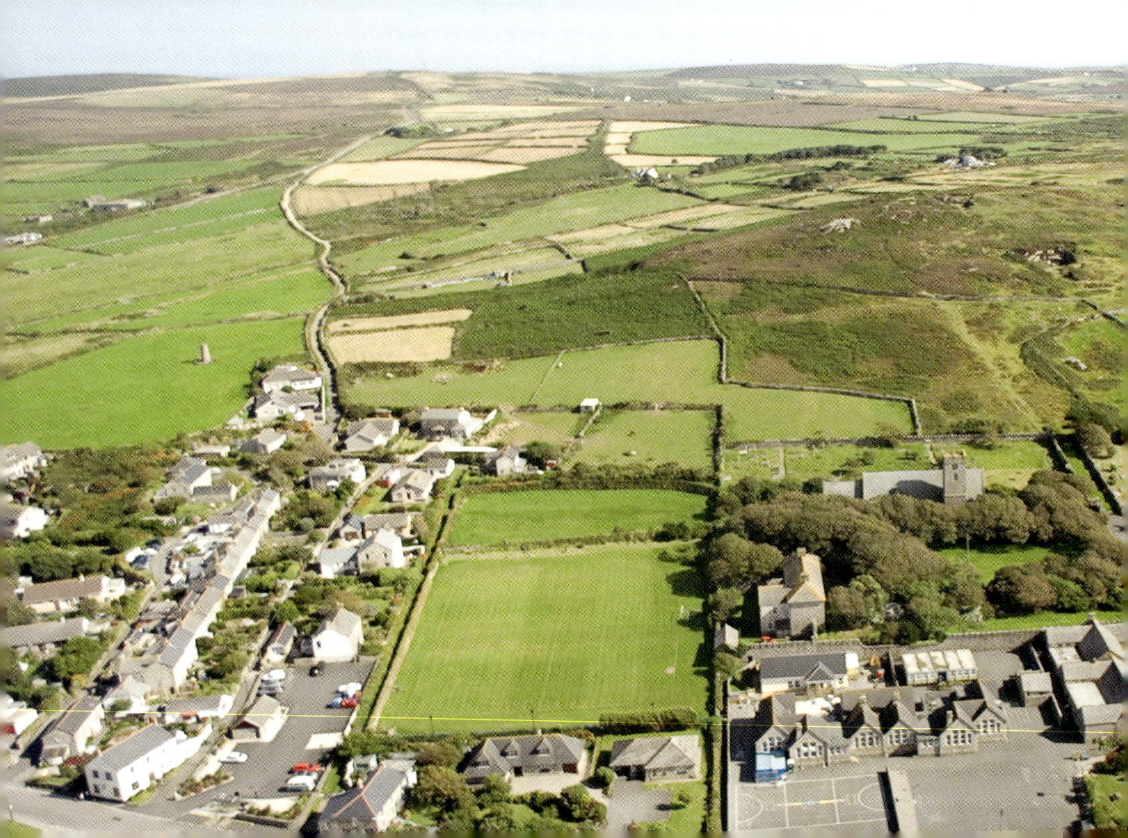

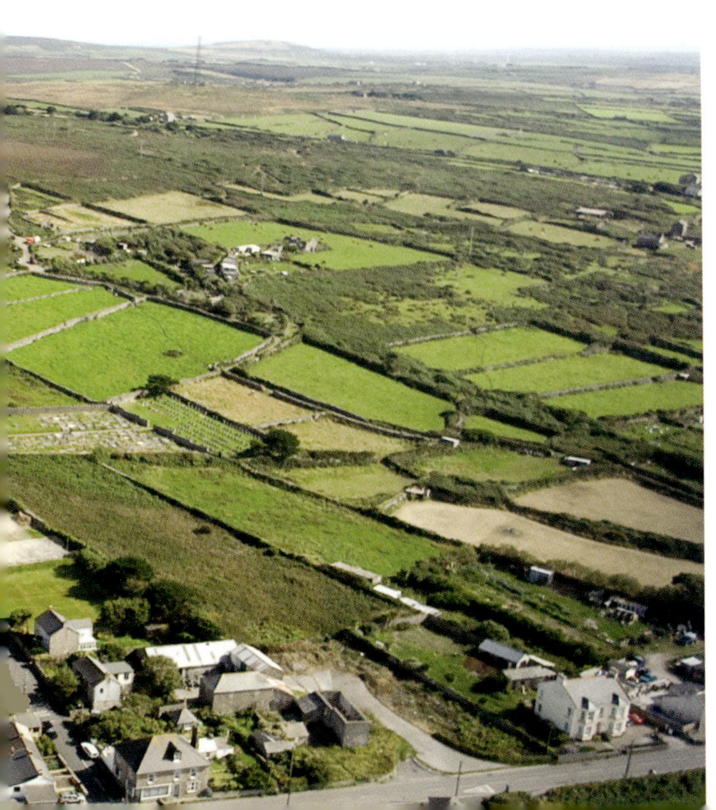

Pendeen, with a view to the moors of Penwith to the south.

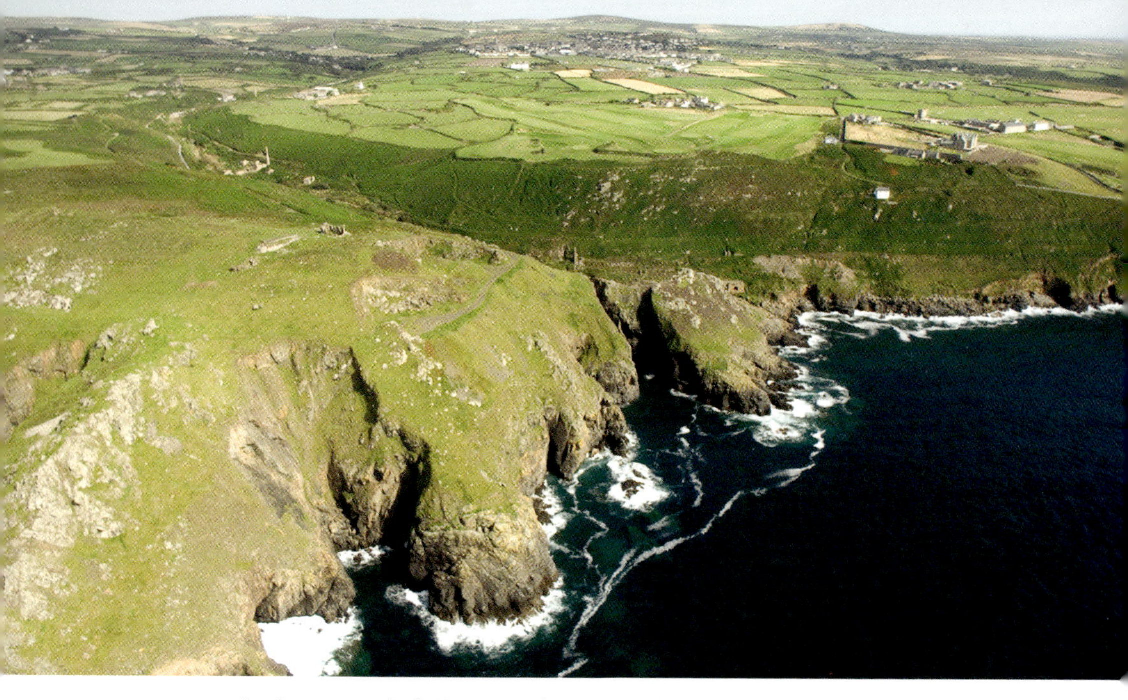

Looking towards St Just over the steep-sided valley at Kenidjack.

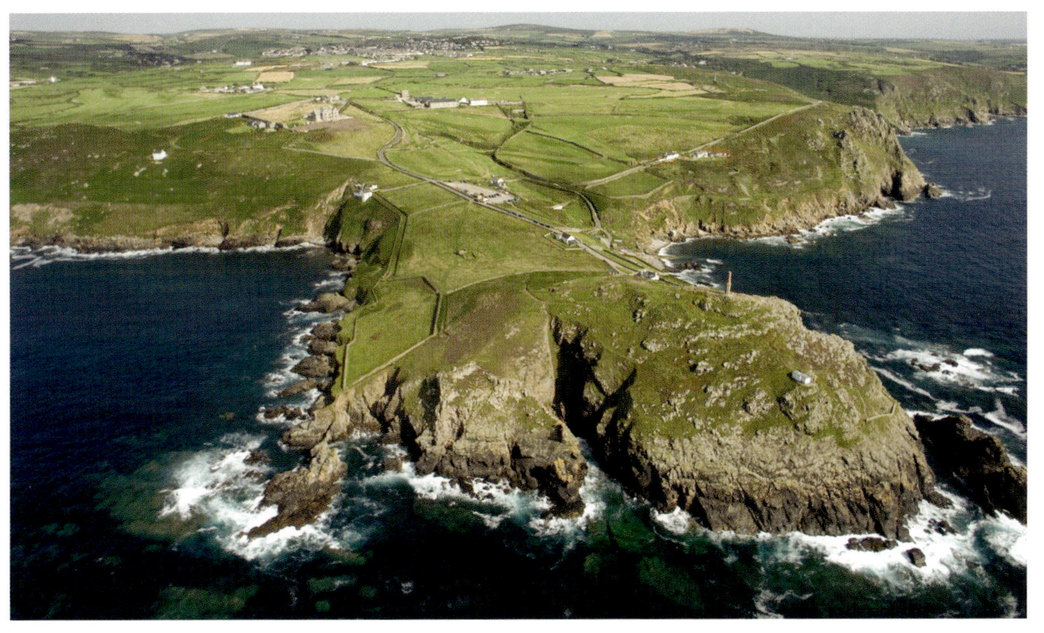

The Sentinel, a brick tower used as a landmark by mariners, stands on Cape Cornwall.

Sennen Cove and lifeboat station.

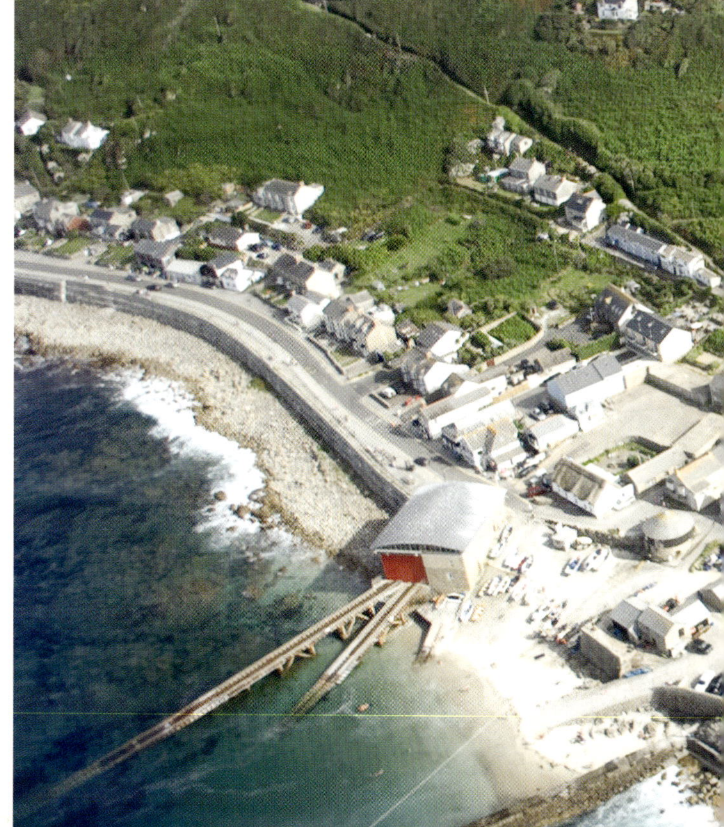

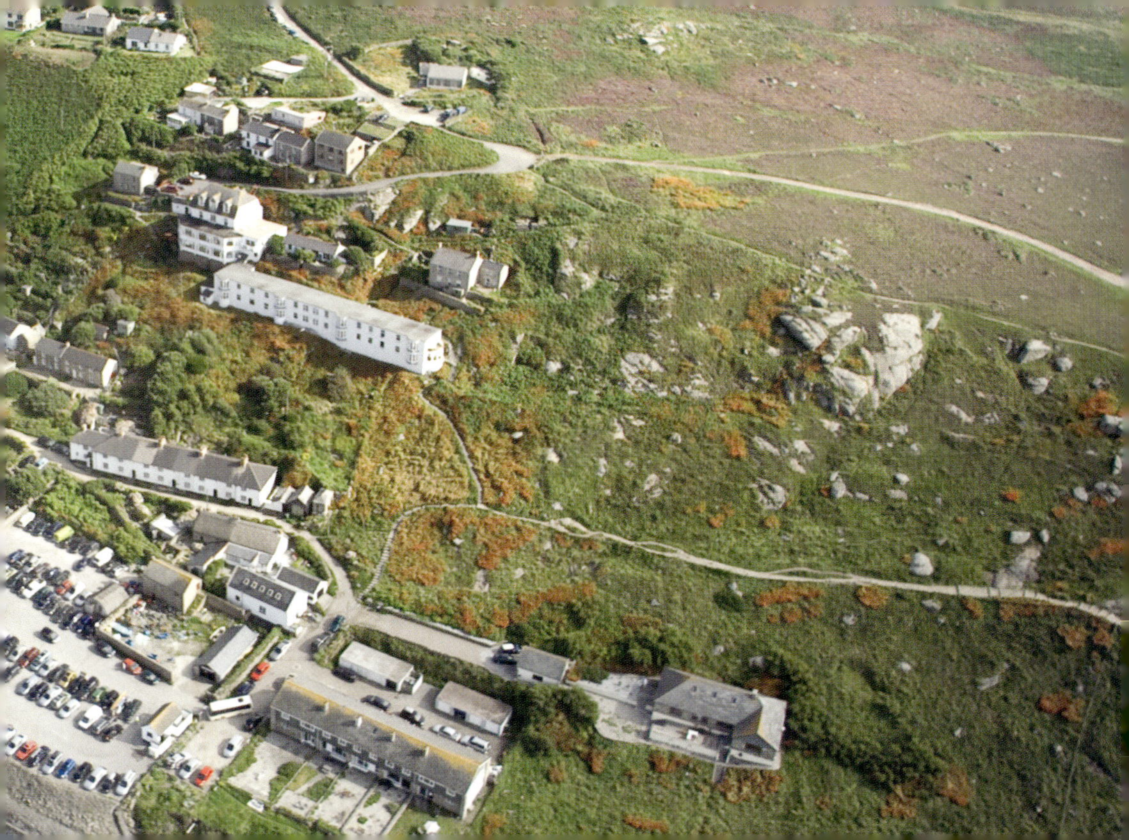

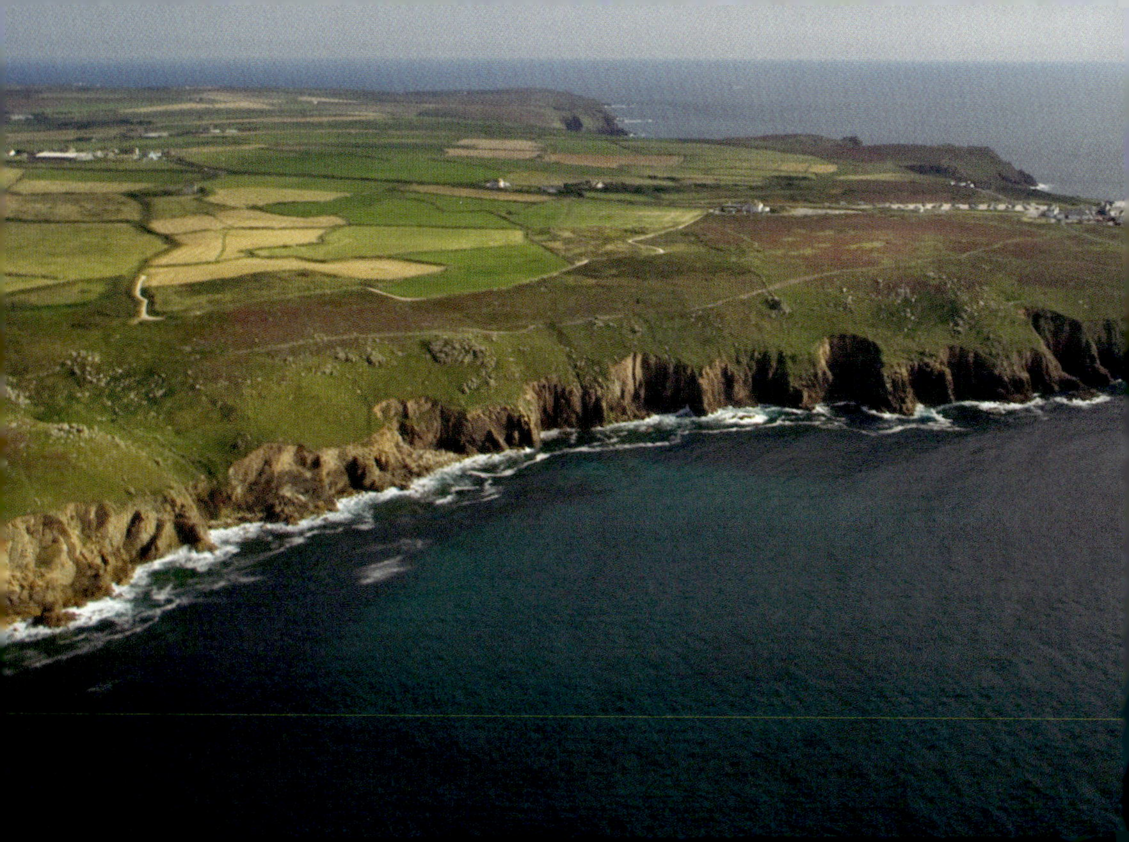

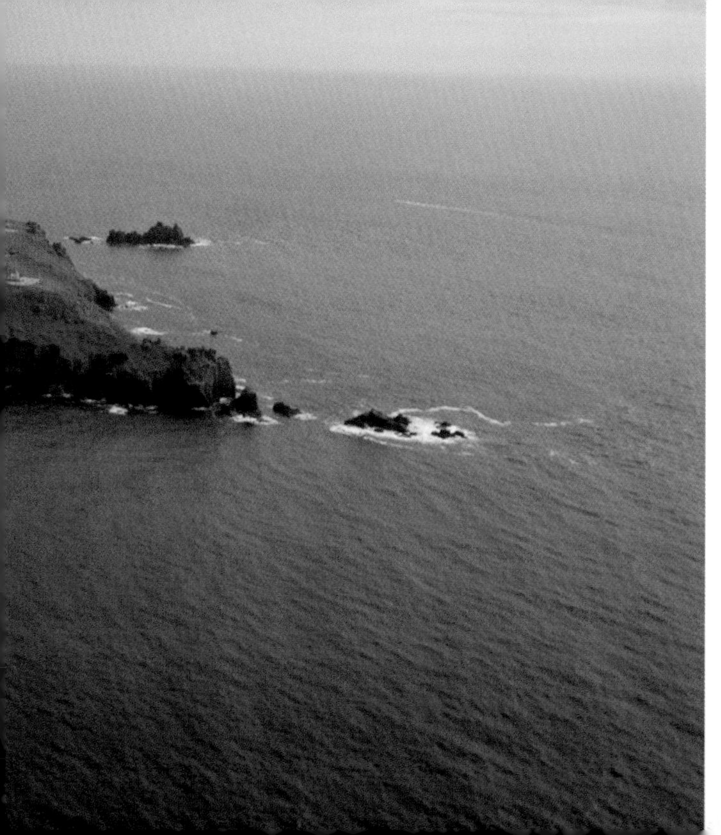

Land's End.

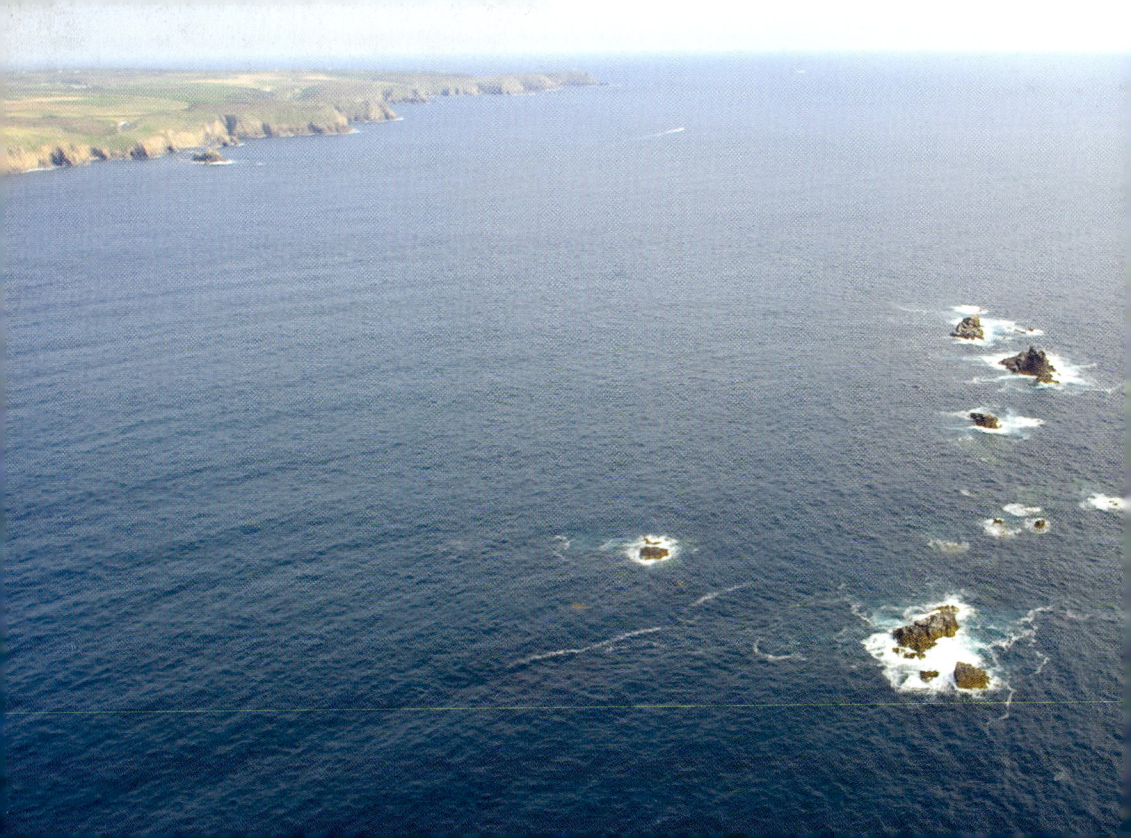

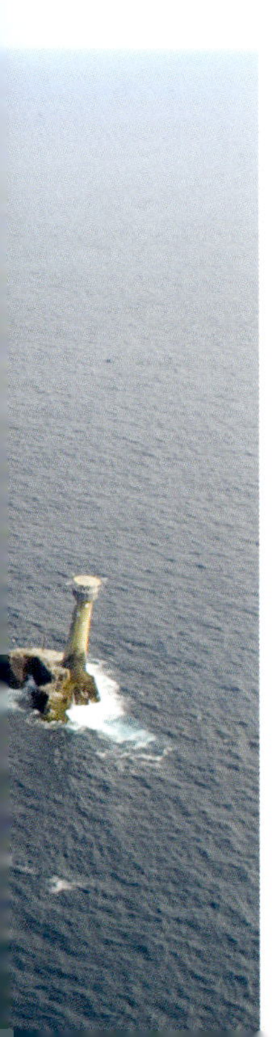

The Longships lighthouse.

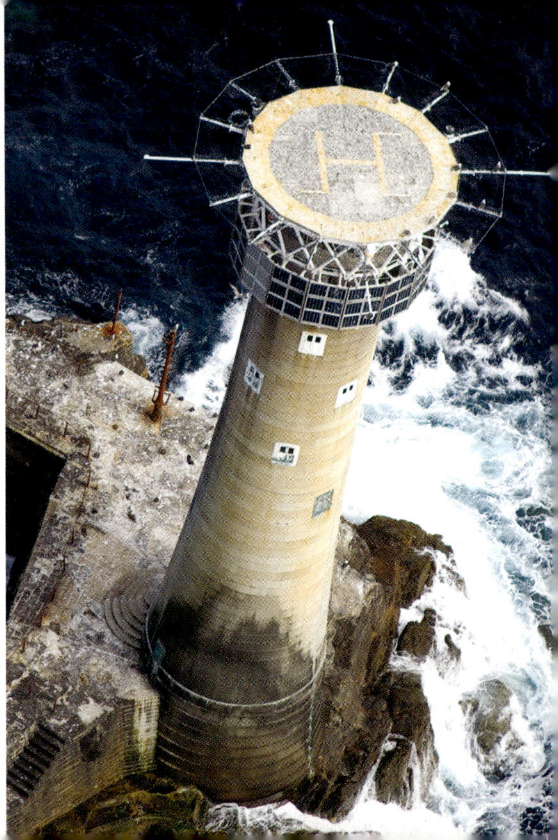

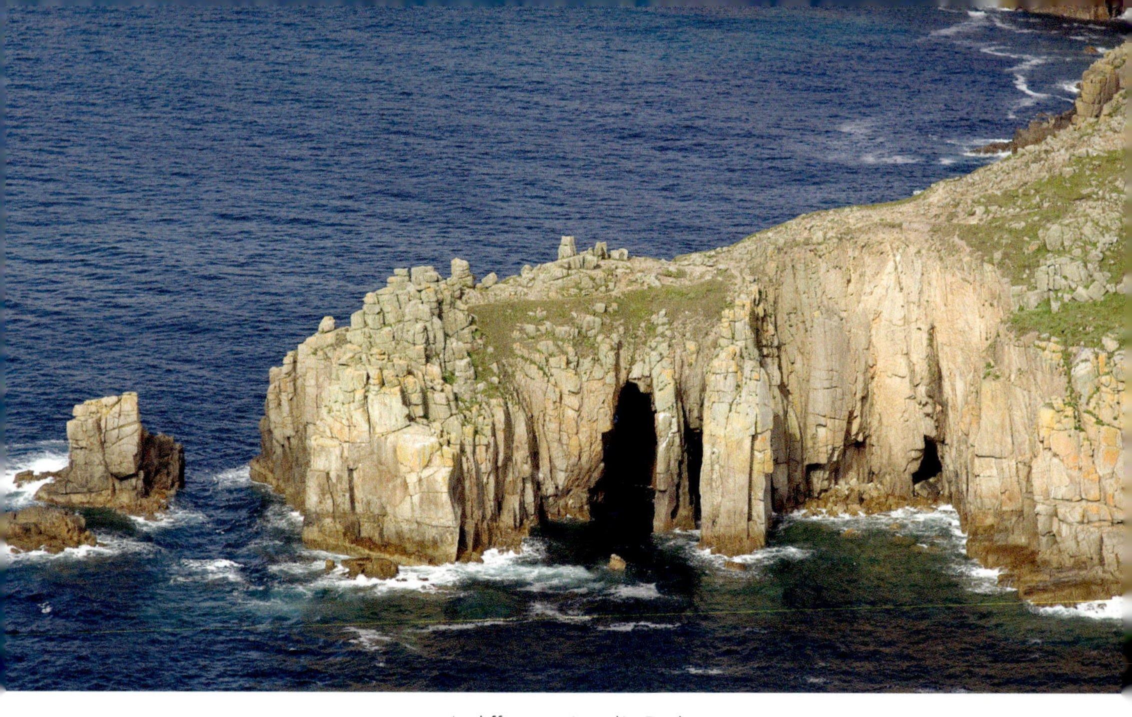

A cliff cave, Land's End.

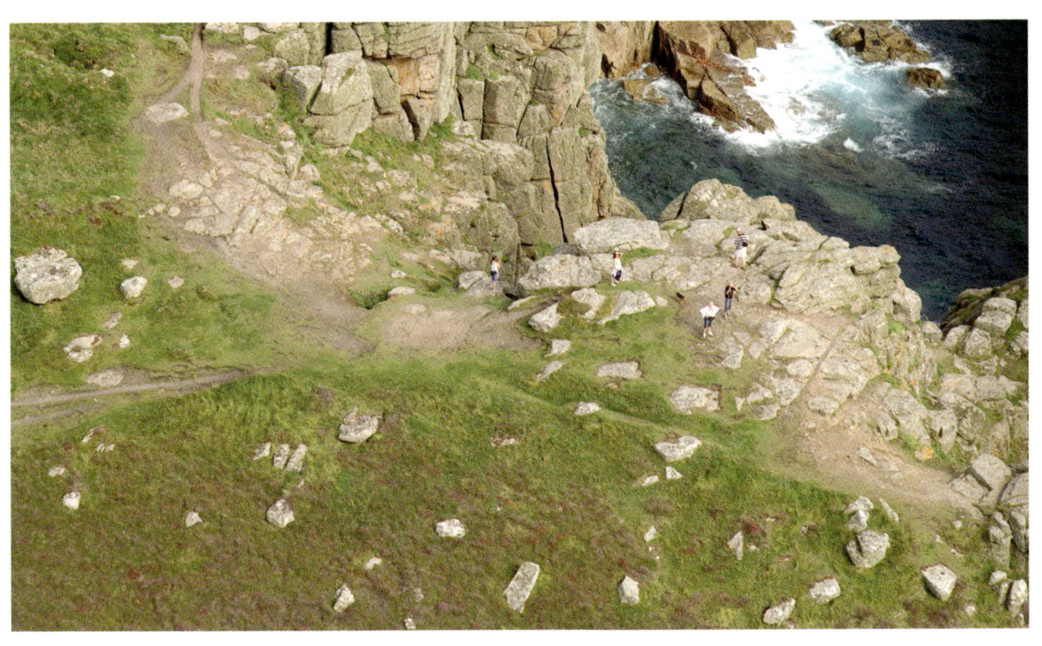

Land's End draws thousands of visitors each year.

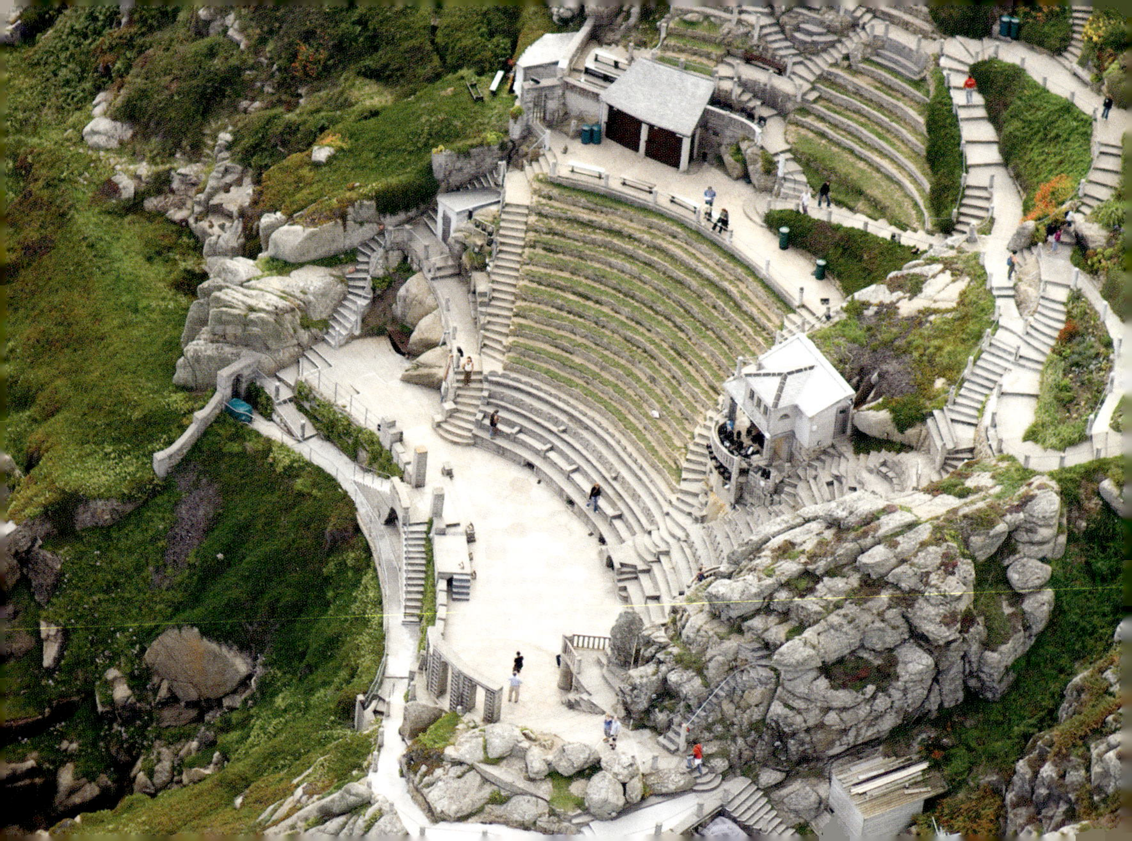

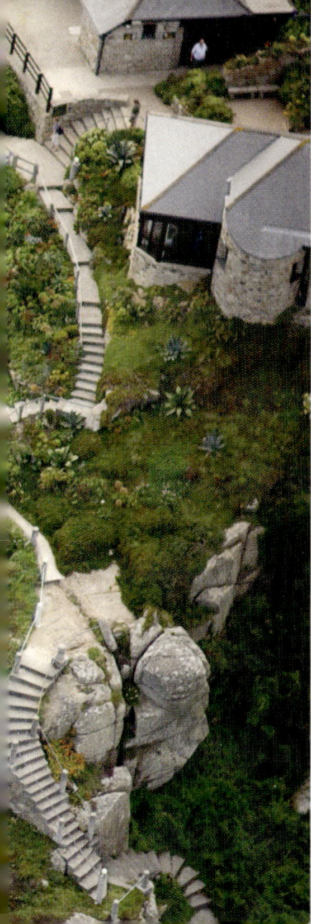

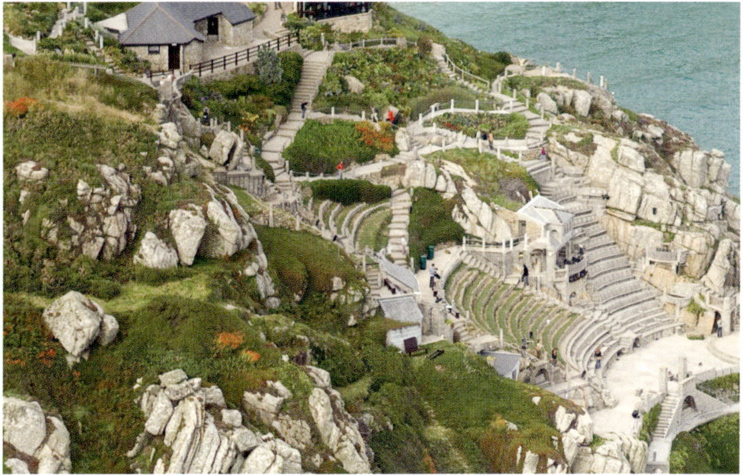

The Minack Theatre.

Opposite:
The spectacular position of the theatre on the cliffs near Porthcurno provides one of the world's most breathtaking theatrical venues.

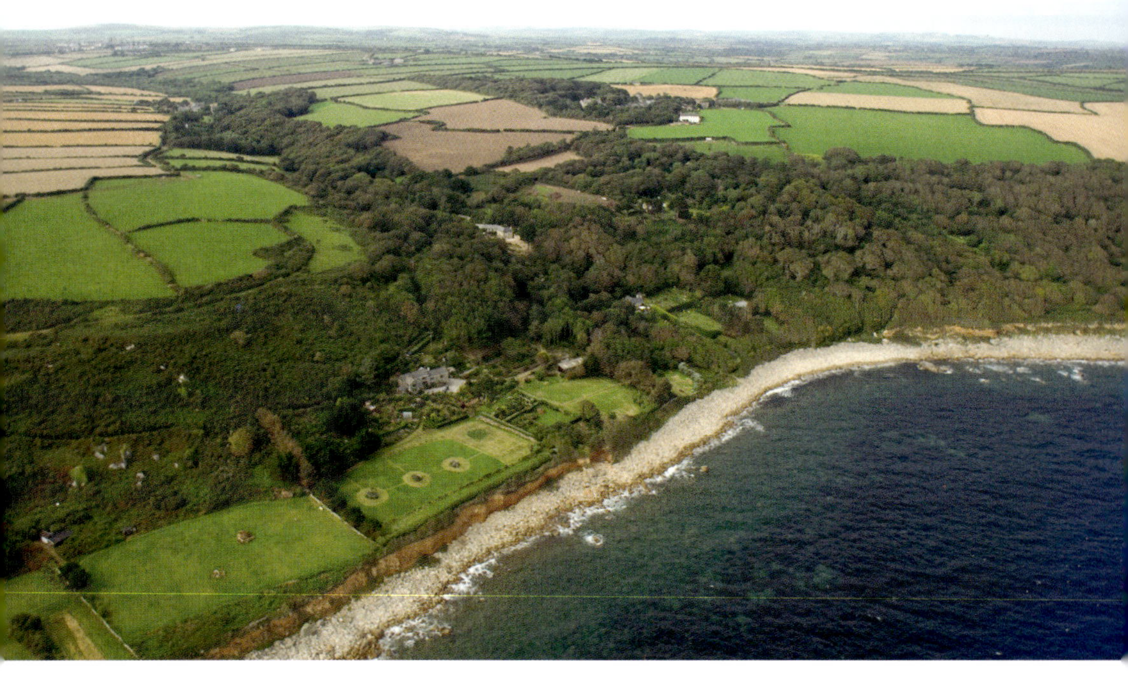

Overlooking St Loy's Cove between Treen and Lamorna.

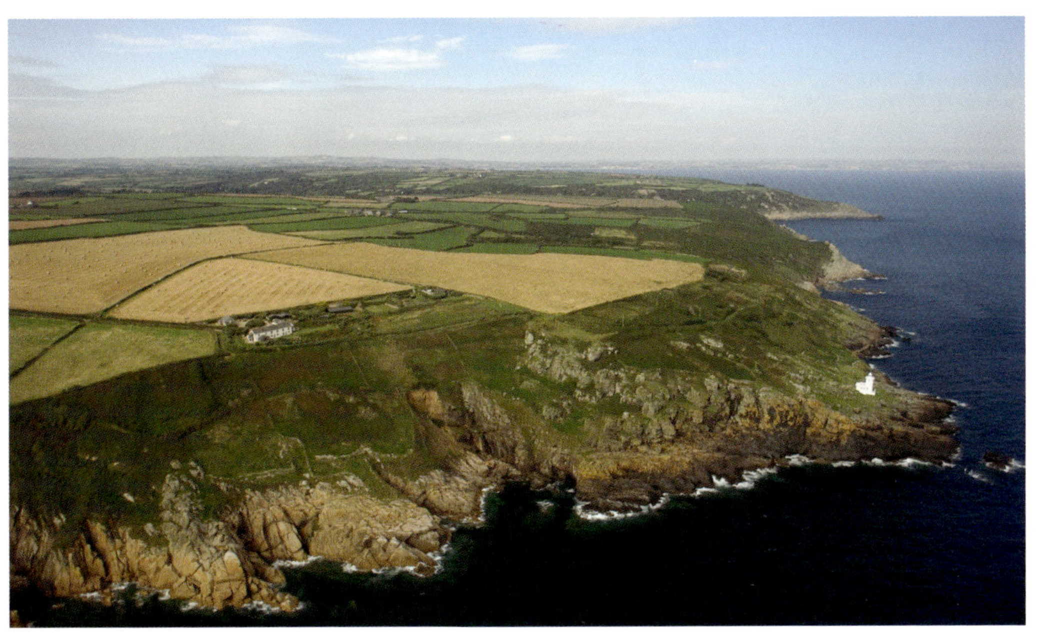

The view north-east, with Mount's Bay in the distance. The lighthouse at Tater Du is the last to be built in Cornwall, constructed in 1965.

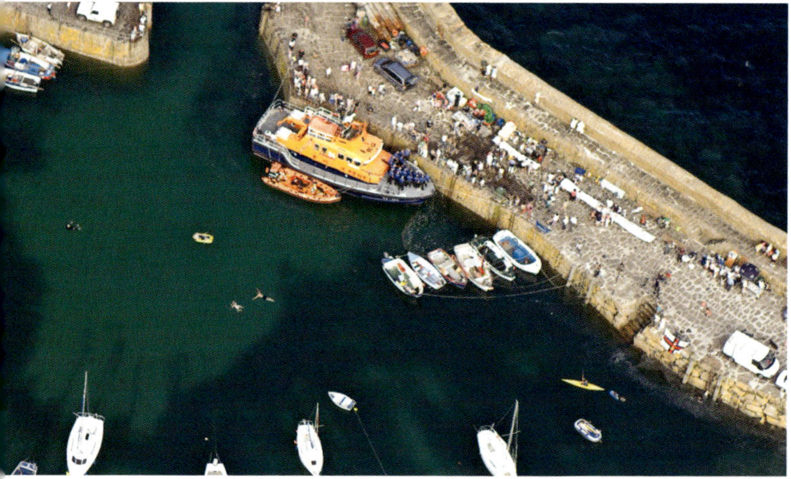

The lifeboat crew chat to the crowds
on the quayside at Mousehole.

Opposite:
Penzance with the Lido and harbour beyond.

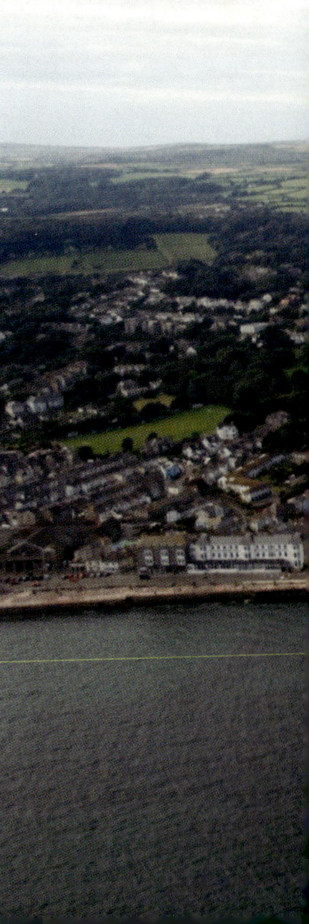

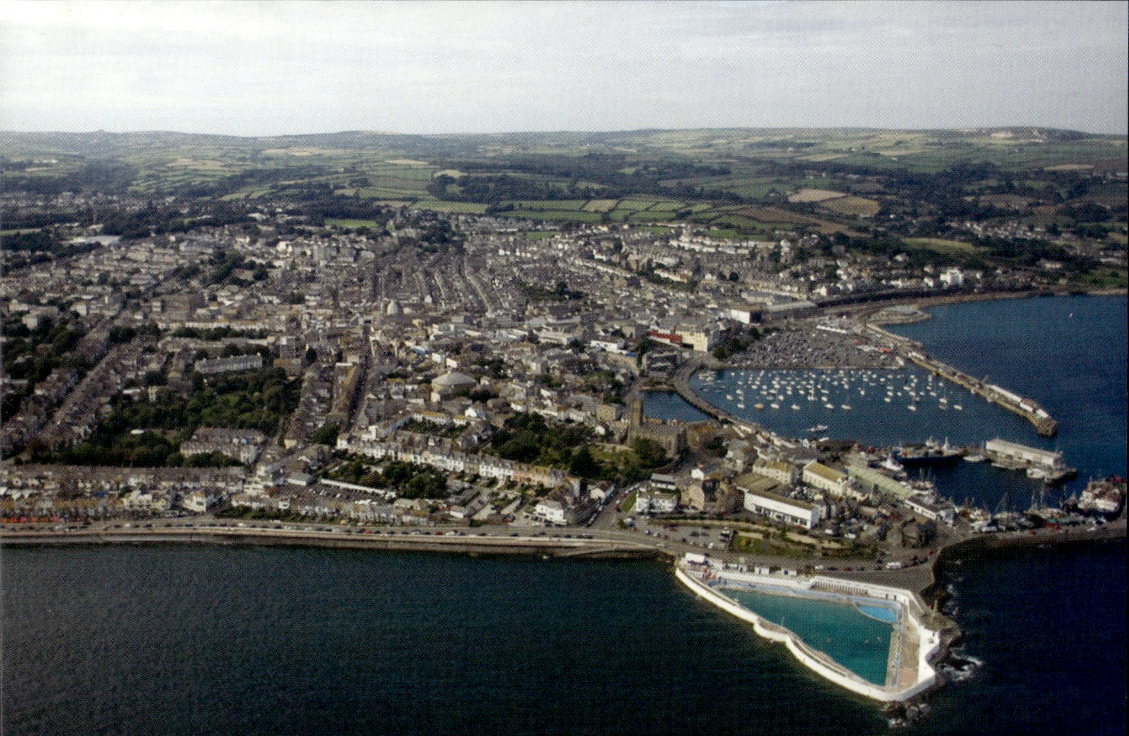

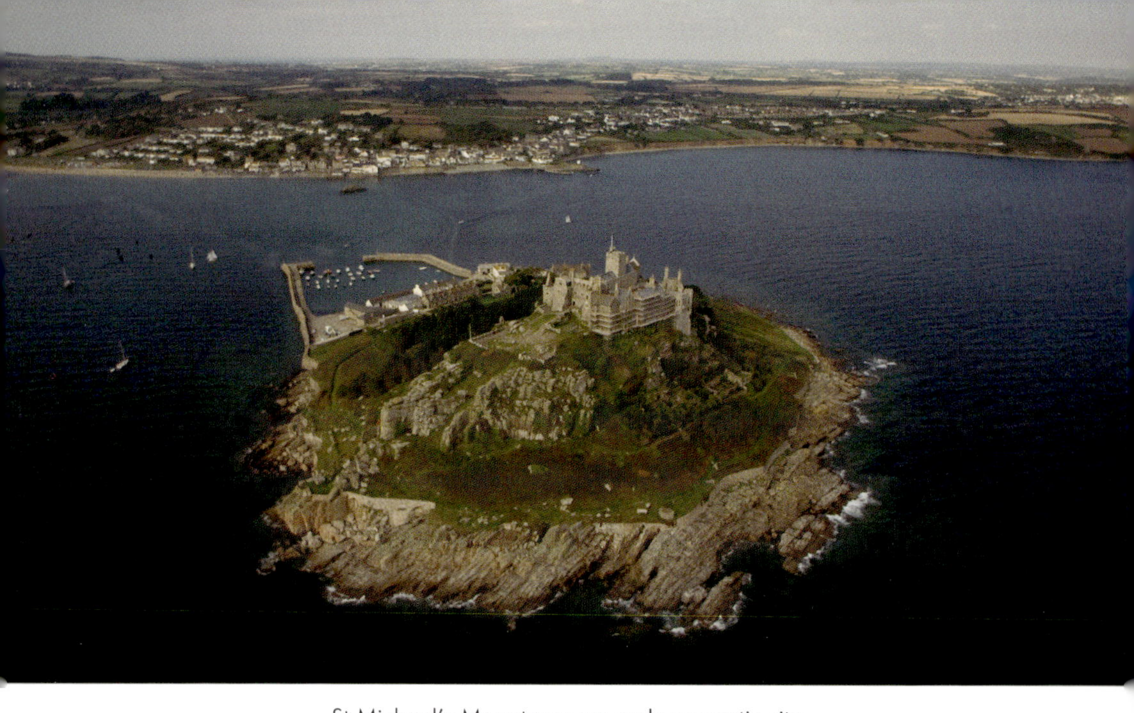

St Michael's Mount was an early monastic site.

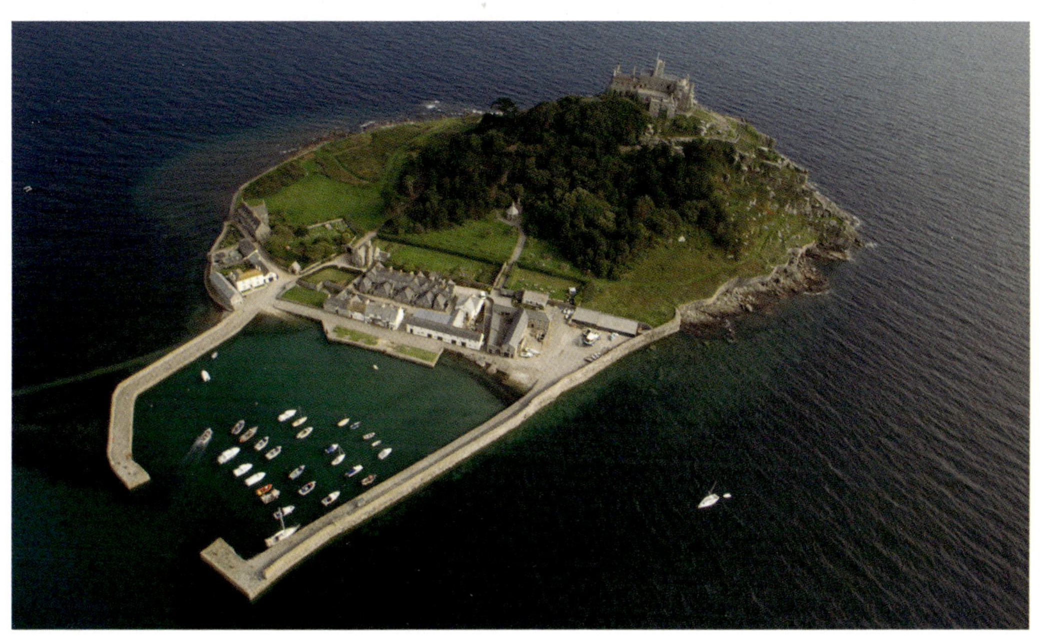

At low tide a causeway connects the island to the mainland at Marazion.

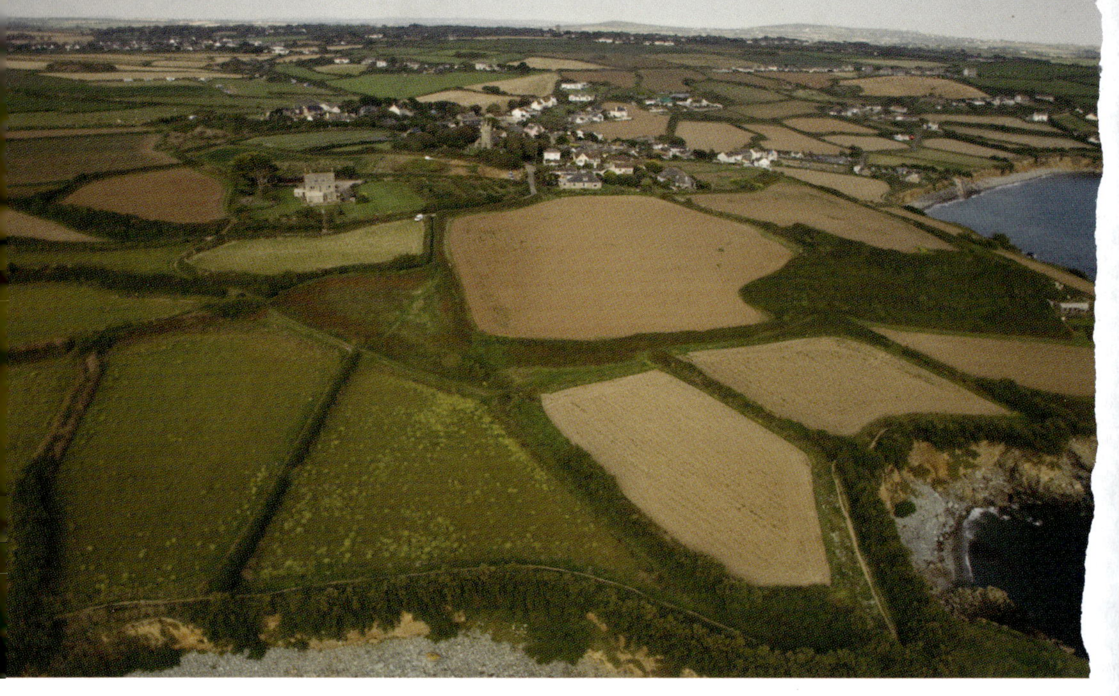

Perranuthnoe marks the boundary of Penwith on Cornwall's southern coast.